Journal for the Evangelical Study of the Old Testament

JESOT is published bi-annually online at www.jesot.org and in print by Wipf and Stock Publishers.
199 West 8th Avenue, Suite 3, Eugene, OR 97401, USA

ISSN 2169-0685
ISBN 978-1-4982-8771-5

© 2015 by Wipf and Stock Publishers

JESOT is an international, peer-reviewed journal devoted to the academic and evangelical study of the Old Testament. The journal seeks to publish current academic research in the areas of ancient Near Eastern backgrounds, Dead Sea Scrolls, Rabbinics, Linguistics, Septuagint, Research Methodology, Literary Analysis, Exegesis, Text Criticism, and Theology as they pertain only to the Old Testament. The journal seeks to provide a venue for high-level scholarship on the Old Testament from an evangelical standpoint. The journal is not affiliated with any particular academic institution, and with an international editorial board, online format, and multi-language submissions, *JESOT* seeks to cultivate Old Testament scholarship in the evangelical global community.

JESOT is indexed in *Old Testament Abstracts*, *Christian Periodical Index*, The Ancient World Online (AWOL), and *EBSCO* databases

Journal for the Evangelical Study of the Old Testament

Executive Editor
STEPHEN J. ANDREWS
(Midwestern Baptist Theological Seminary, USA)

Editor
WILLIAM R. OSBORNE
(College of the Ozarks, USA)

Associate Editor
RUSSELL L. MEEK
(Louisiana College, USA)

Journal correspondence and manuscript submissions should be directed to editor@jesot.org. Instructions for authors can be found at www.jesot.org.

Books for review and review correspondence should be directed to Russell Meek at rmeek@jesot.org.

All ordering and subscription inquiries should be sent to Orders@wipfandstock.com.

Editorial Board

T. DESMOND ALEXANDER (Union Theological College, Queens University, Ireland)

GEORGE ATHAS (Moore College, Australia)

ELLIS R. BROTZMAN (Emeritus, Tyndale Theological Seminary, The Netherlands)

HÉLÈNE DALLAIRE (Denver Seminary, USA)

JOHN F. EVANS (Nairobi Evangelical Graduate School of Theology, Kenya)

KYLE GREENWOOD (Colorado Christian University, USA)

JOHN HOBBINS (University of Wisconsin – Oshkosh, USA)

JERRY HWANG (Singapore Bible College, Singapore)

JENS BRUUN KOFOED (Fjellhaug International University College, Denmark)

KENNETH A. MATHEWS (Beeson Divinty School, Samford University, USA)

CRISTIAN RATA (Torch Trinity Graduate University, South Korea)

MATHIEU RICHELLE (Faculté Libre de Théologie Évangélique, France)

MAX ROGLAND (Erskine Theological Seminary, USA)

LENA-SOFIA TIEMEYER (University of Aberdeen, Scotland)

BARRY G. WEBB (Emeritus, Moore College, Australia

THE ANTIOCH BIBLE
THE SYRIAC PESHITTA BIBLE WITH ENGLISH TRANSLATION

"[Early Syriac Christianity] offers us a largely unhellenized form of Christianity that is deeply Biblical in character and quite different in many respects from the Christianity of the Greek- and Latin-speaking world of the Mediterranean littoral."
—*Sebastian Brock (University of Oxford)*

The Antioch Bible is a new, easy-to-read translation of the Syriac Peshitta Bible, a Middle Eastern version of Scripture that dates back to the early days of Christianity. This translation is the work of an international, interfaith team of scholars from North America and Europe.

Syriac, the language of the Peshitta, is a dialect of Aramaic similar to the language of the Jewish exile and the Palestinian Aramaic of Jesus Christ, and used by Jews and Christians throughout the Middle East for centuries. The Old Testament, which preserves differences not found in either Greek or Hebrew, is rich with links to the ancient Jewish exegetical tradition, while the New Testament can help uncover the original Semitic thoughts underlying the Greek words.

Illuminating Variant Readings

The high places of Isaac shall be made desolate, and the sanctuaries of Israel shall be laid waste, and I will rise against the house of Jerobo'am with the sword.
—*Amos 7:9, Revised Standard Version*

The ridiculous idols' shrines will be laid waste, the sanctuaries of Israel will be laid waste, I will arise against the house of Jeroboam with the sword.
—*Amos 7:9, Syriac Peshitta*

What are the "high places of Isaac"? In this example, the Hebrew is unclear. The Syriac version not only demystifies the Hebrew vocabulary but also fits the verse to its context.

Cloth-bound editions, printed on matte paper with ornate end sheets

---

Limited time offer for JESOT readers
Lock in your subscription rate at $75/volume*, 50% off the list price!
*Institutions may subscribe at $100/volume

Visit www.gorgiaspress.com/AntiochBible for more information

Allusions to the Levitical Leprosy Laws in the Jericho Narratives (Joshua 2 and 6)

NICHOLAS P. LUNN

Wycliffe Bible Translators and Spurgeon's College, London
nick_lunn@sil.org

This article explores one particular case in which a narrative of the Old Testament historical books references laws within the legal code of Israel. The particular manner of intertextual relationship in question is that of allusion rather than direct citation. Following a discussion of how the Deuteromonic History was familiar with contents of the Priestly Code, it is here argued that in composing his account of the spying out of Jericho and its subsequent overthrow, the author of the book of Joshua was looking to the levitical laws regarding leprosy to help enhance his narrative in a meaningful way. All three categories of leprous infection (of a person, a house, and a garment) dealt with in the law have their counterparts in the historical account. When viewed against the backdrop of the Hebrews occupying a land inhabited by Canaanites, each of the three cases delivers an appropriate message to Israel.

KEYWORDS: *leprosy, Jericho, Rahab, Deuteronomic History, Leviticus, Priestly Code, allusion, intertextuality*

KNOWLEDGE OF THE LAW IN THE DEUTERONOMIC HISTORY

That the books of the Deuteronomic History should make reference to laws within the Deuteronomic code is a fact that requires no substantiation. The whole point of the designation lies in the foundation of the historical books in question upon that body of legal material. At times the manner of reference is obvious, as in the case of the injunction to conduct a ceremony of blessings and curses at the mountains of Ebal and Gerizim (Deut 11:29; 27:12–13; cf. Josh 8:30–35). Occasionally, however, the manner of reference is more allusive. It is demonstrable that the two accounts of Joshua hanging various Canaanite kings on trees until the evening (Josh 8:29; 10:26) alludes to the law found in Deut 21:22–23.[1] Further, the narrative relating Israel's request for a king from the prophet Samuel (1 Sam 8:4–20) can be seen to allude to the law occurring in Deut 21:14–17.[2]

Attention is less frequently drawn to the fact that the Deuteronomic History also shows familiarity with events and even laws appearing in the other parts of the Pentateuch outside of Deuteronomy. The writers of the history show an obvious general acquaintance with the roles of the priests (Josh 6:4) and Levites (Josh 21:1), the tabernacle (Josh 22:19), the ark of the covenant (Judg 20:27), lampstand (1 Sam 3:3), ephod (1 Sam 2:28), as well as the Urim and Thummim (1 Sam 28:6). Yet in addition to this general knowledge of such matters, certain passages reveal a close familiarity with more precise details, as shall be demonstrated.

In certain instances the connection between the history and the law seems to be conclusive from the wording used, as in the matter relating to the daughters of Zelophedad, where almost exact repetition occurs (Josh 17.3; cf. Num 26.33). The same would apply to Samson's status as a Nazirite, where the book of Judges (13:5–7) betrays knowledge of the vow recorded in Numbers (6:1–8). Together with the use of the actual term "Nazirite" (נזיר), the prohibitions regarding the consumption of alcohol (יין ושכר in both cases), and the cutting of hair ("no razor shall pass/come upon his head") argue for interdependence.

Of greater relevance for our present purposes is the evidence that points to knowledge of certain aspects of the levitical legislation on the part of those who wrote the history. A close study shows that this is the inescapable conclusion. And it is even sometimes seen to be that where a corresponding law exists within Deuteronomy, the form of the reference in the history at the verbal level relates more closely to that found in Leviticus. This is so, for example, with the prohibition against consuming blood. The laws concerning this are alluded to in 1 Sam 14:32–34, recording the occasion when, during the pursuit of their enemies, the men of Israel stopped to feed on meat containing blood. Deuteronomy forbids such a practice (12:15–25; 15:22–23). Yet, a study of the language employed in the Samuel account shows that the author's wording exhibits greater similarity to the prohibition in its levitical form (Lev 17:10–14; 19:26). There are several linguistic details that put this beyond

---

1. Cf. David M. Howard, *Joshua: An Exegetical and Theological Exposition of Holy Scripture* (NAC 5; Nashville: Broadman & Holman, 1998), 211.

2. Cf. Robert P. Gordon, *1 and 2 Samuel: A Commentary* (LBI; Grand Rapids: Zondervan, 1986), 110.

doubt. First, the verbal phrase "eat with the blood," occurring twice in the narrative (1 Sam 14:32, ויאכל העם על־הדם; v. 33, לאכל על־הדם), is that appearing in Leviticus (19:26, לא תאכלו על־הדם) and not at all in Deuteronomy. Second, the verb for slaughtering the animals is שחט, found three times in the narrative (1 Sam 14:32, וישחטו; v. 34, ושחטתם, וישחטו), and twice in the relevant levitical prohibition (Lev 17:3, ישחט). This particular verb does not appear even once in Deuteronomy, not just in the blood laws, but anywhere in the entire book. Third, the specific animals mentioned in the context are "ox or sheep" (1 Sam 14:34), which corresponds closely to "ox, lamb, or goat" of the levitical law (Lev 17:3). The animals in both the Deuteronomic versions of the law, however, are the "gazelle and the deer" (Deut 12:15, 22; 15:22).

A similar phenomenon is observable in Saul's prohibition of mediums and spiritists. This is mentioned twice and in both cases the form and order of terms is האבות then הידענים (1 Sam 28:3, 9). The use of two plural nouns and the order are identical to what is found in the two laws in Leviticus (19:31; 20:6). In both the narrative and the levitical injunctions, these two are the only types of offender listed. In Deuteronomy, however, the law is somewhat different. Besides using singular nominal phrases, the two corresponding persons are merely part of a much longer list of those prohibited: "There shall not be found among you anyone who makes his son or his daughter pass through the fire, one who uses divination, one who practices witchcraft, or one who interprets omens, or a sorcerer, or one who casts a spell, or a medium, or a spiritist, or one who consults the dead" (Deut 18:10–11). More than this, here in Hebrew the phrase "medium, or a spiritist" is in fact a circumlocution, שאל אוב וידעני, that is, one "who consults ghosts or spirits" (NRSV). So again, in a range of details we find that the historical book more closely echoes the form of the law in Leviticus.

Further evidence of a similar nature could be adduced from the purification of Bathsheba, where the phrase "consecrating herself from her uncleanness" (2 Sam 11:4) is evidently levitical in character, as Leviticus (16:19) contains the only other use of the phrase in the whole of Hebrew scripture. Likewise, the cleansing of Naaman the leper involves him having to wash himself in the Jordan seven times. It is surely not merely a coincidence that the levitical leprosy laws include the sprinkling of the one with leprosy seven times with water and blood as part of the cleansing ritual (Lev 14:7)

The purpose of this paper is not to offer an account for the dependence shown above. Suffice it to say that a variety of explanations present themselves. First, both the historical books and the priestly material may have reached their final form around the same period, which some would claim to be the exilic or postexilic, and the allusions to the priestly legislation may have been introduced into the history by the latter's final redactor(s). Second, while the historical writings may be of a significantly earlier date than the final encoding of the priestly, a certain amount of the latter was already partially in circulation, possibly in oral form, or in shorter documents that would later form a source basis for the code. A third alternative is the traditional view regarding the books attributed to Moses, which is that the composition of these predated that of the historical books.

Whichever of the foregoing explanations is adopted, each allows the possible scenario in which we may encounter a narrative within the Deuteronomic History that echoes one of the levitical laws. Whether at that time the content of the law was accessible only orally, or through fragmentary sources, or through a complete written code of earlier or contemporary date, the fact evidently remains that it was accessible.

In what follows certain details appearing in the passages of the book of Joshua relating to the fall of Jericho are identified as establishing a previously undetected connection with the levitical laws dealing with leprosy (Lev 13–14). This is an instance in which the historical book, rather than cite, refers to the legal material in a more subtle manner by way of allusions of a linguistic and thematic nature.

THE LEVITICAL LAWS REGARDING LEPROSY

The instructions found in Lev 13–14 are lengthy and complex. It is not my intention to unravel the numerous details given there. This would be quite unnecessary since these laws are not being applied to the situation occurring in Joshua, but rather literary allusions are being created. Here it will suffice only to provide an outline and summary of the laws, and to highlight a number of specific features.

The two chapters present procedures relating to certain infections that affect not only humans, but inanimate objects also. The precise nature of the various conditions being described is not easy to establish in each case. There are commentaries that offer substantial discussion of such matters, to which the reader may resort.[3] All that will be noted here is that the same general Hebrew term (צרעת) is used throughout, regardless of who or what it actually is that suffers from the condition (e.g., 13:2; 14:7, 34). This term has traditionally been rendered "leprosy." While it may seem incongruous to modern medical science for the same diagnosis to be applied to both persons and objects, that is how

---

3. E.g., Gordon J. Wenham, *The Book of Leviticus* (NICOT; Grand Rapids: Eerdmans, 1979), 194–97.

the Hebrews used the term. As the present article does not require an exact understanding of any of the conditions involved, I will simply follow the Hebrew practice and refer to each of its particular manifestations as "leprosy."

This part of Leviticus contains four basic literary units that deal with the identification of leprosy and related diseases and the consequent procedures with respect to three distinct categories:

(1) Regulations regarding an infected person (13:1–46; 14:1–32).
(2) Regulations regarding an infected fabric (13:47–59).
(3) Regulations regarding an infected house (14:33–53).

Whereas the instructions regarding fabrics and houses include all the various elements in a single block of text, in the case of persons the cleansing ceremony is treated separately (14:1–32). In each instance the possibility is allowed that the infection may cease, though in none of the three cases is an explanation given as to how this may occur. Should the disease remain, the consequence is continued separation for a person (13:46), burning for a fabric (13:52, 57), and the pulling down of the infected house (14:45).

There are two further details to which attention ought to be drawn. The first of these is the leading role of the priests. The application of the various regulations falls wholly to the direction of a priest (referred to more than 70 times in the two chapters). This fact, and the lack of mention of any doctor or healing methods, suggests the basis of the laws lies in ceremonial factors rather than medical. It does not appear that the treatment and care of lepers is primarily in view, though these were no doubt a matter for social concern in ancient Israel. Rather it is the state of cleanness and uncleanness caused by such conditions and how reinstatement to the former may be obtained that is of principal importance.[4]

Second, there is the marked use of time phrases involved in the different procedures. To be more precise, there is one single time reference that is repeated at regular intervals, which is that of seven days (18 times in total—13:4, 5, 6, 21, 22, 26, 27, 31, 32, 33, 34, 50, 51, 54; 14:8, 9, 38, 39). Besides these more prominent features, other lesser details occurring in these laws will receive attention as we proceed.

---

4. Cf. ibid., 203.

The Leprous House

From a close reading of the Jericho narratives in the book of Joshua it becomes evident that the author was making deliberate allusion to the above laws. To his mind a manner of analogy existed, in the first instance, between the city in question and the leprous house treated in those laws.

The two relevant historical narratives are found in Josh 2:1–24 and 6:1–27. While not forming a consecutive account in that the crossing of the Jordan intervenes, the two are obviously thematically related. In the earlier of the narratives the city is spied out, in the later it is destroyed. In the former a promise is made to Rahab and her family, in the latter they are delivered from the city according to that same promise.

It is in connection with the opening of the second narrative that one of the more obvious allusions to the leprosy laws occurs. This passage begins with the statement: "Now Jericho was firmly shut up [סגרת ומסגרת] because of the Israelites; no one went out and no one came in" (6:1). The double use of the verb סגר is striking. This same verb is also prominent in Lev 13–14, where it occurs eleven times (13:4, 5, 11, 21, 26, 31, 33, 50, 54; 14:38, 46). There it is used for the act of separating an infected person (e.g., 13:4), or, more significantly, for shutting up an infected house (14:38). The basic meaning of the verb is simply "to shut," yet in the context of leprosy it takes on the more technical sense of "isolate" or "segregate." Interestingly, in the literary arrangement of the Hexateuch, the sole occurrences of this particular verb between the regulations of Lev 13–14 and the book of Joshua is in Num 12, also dealing with the subject matter of leprosy, this time pertaining to Miriam who had been afflicted with the disease (vv. 14, 15). סגר is a word then that could readily acquire connotations of leprosy.

How can we be certain that the usage in Josh 6:1 is allusive and not merely coincidental? Other considerations place the deliberateness beyond question. The infected house that is "shut up" in Lev 14 has undergone previous examination. A priest had been called that "he should come [יבא] to view [לראות] the house" (14:36; cf. v. 37, וראה, v. 44, וראה . . . ובא). In the first of the two narratives in Joshua the two spies are instructed by their leader to "Go, view [ראו] the land" (2:1). Shortly after their arrival in Jericho it becomes known to the men of the city that the two had "come [באו] to spy out the land" (2:2, 3).[5] It is subsequent to this prior coming and viewing in both contexts that leads to the place

---

5. In each text, therefore, we find a verb of seeing or viewing adjoined to a verb of motion.

being shut up.

The connection is further established through the presence of a seven-day period in each instance. Lev 14:38 immediately qualifies the acting of shutting up the house with the temporal phrase "for seven days." The statement in Josh 6:1 about Jericho being shut is immediately followed by the instructions of God to Joshua concerning a seven-day period (vv. 2–5), during which, by inference, the city will remain in its shut-up condition. This seven-day period, the prominence of which in the leprosy laws was noted above, is mentioned again in vv. 15–16. Ostensibly the whole affair respecting Israel before Jericho was structured around this particular span of time.

Alongside the seven-day period we find in both texts an action performed seven times. The purification ritual for the infected house involves it being sprinkled with sacrificial blood "seven times [שֶׁבַע פְּעָמִים]" (Lev 14:51), a phrase appearing in other leprosy rituals (14:7, 16, 29). At Jericho the Israelites are instructed to march around the city "seven times [שֶׁבַע פְּעָמִים]" (Josh 6:4). The priests are, moreover, mentioned in both these verses, and are key participants in Joshua 6 generally (nine times—vv. 4 [twice], 6 [twice], 8, 9, 12, 13, 16), as they are in Lev 13–14. As regards the infected house, the direction of the priest leads to its stones being dismantled (Lev 14:40–45). At Jericho it is a distinctive trumpet-blast by the priests (Josh 6:4–5) that initiates the collapse of the city.

Additionally, there are other less noticeable points of contact. We find that regarding the leprous house "one who enters [וְהַבָּא] . . . shall be unclean" (14:46). With regard to Jericho, Josh 6:1 declares that "there was no one entering [וְאֵין בָּא]." While not identical, there is a clear conceptual interrelation in that both concern restrictions upon entering the place in question. Also, the "wall" of the structure is in each case given its own particular mention. In Lev 14 the walls of the house receive the priest's closest attention (vv. 37, 39) to see if there is any trace of the disease "in the walls" (בְּקִירֹת). In the Jericho narrative, Rahab and her family, who offered shelter to the spies, live "in the wall" (בְּקִיר). In both places we find the same Hebrew term, 2:15 being the sole occurrence of the word קִיר in the entire book of Joshua.

Another more apparent conceptual feature shared by both texts is the ultimate destruction of the edifice in question. If the disease with which the house is contaminated persists, then "the house shall be pulled down, its stones, its timber, and all the plaster of the house" (Lev 14:45). In the case of Jericho, the walls collapse and the city is destroyed (Josh 6:20–21, 24). The ruins of the infected house are deposited in an unclean place (Lev 14:45), while a curse is uttered over the ruins of Jericho (Josh 6:26).

One final detail in this connection is the manner in which the law concerning "leprosy" within a house is introduced. This section begins with the words, "When you enter [תבאו] the land [ארץ] of Canaan, which I am giving you [נתן לכם] ... [אשר] as a possession . . ." (Lev 14:34). By this means the matter concerning such a house is distinctly set within the context of the land promised as a possession. The same obviously holds true for the events at Jericho. Israel is expressly told, "you will cross the Jordan here to enter [לבוא] and take possession of the land [הארץ] the LORD your God is giving you [נתן לכם] ... [אשר] to possess" (Josh 1:11). The similarity of words and ideas is self evident, and it is just a few sentences later than the first part of the Jericho narrative commences (Josh 2:1). Both the law and the narrative are, therefore, placed within a similar geographical setting, namely the land which is being given to Israel as a possession.

Taken together the number and nature of the foregoing correspondences between the two loci suggest that the author of one was purposely creating allusions to the other. Such a conclusion is supported by other considerations to follow.

THE LEPROUS PERSON

Much of the levitical legislation regarding leprosy involves the disease affecting people. The diagnosis is treated extensively in Lev 13:1–46, and the associated purification rituals are in 14:1–32. Just as the author of Joshua established connections between the law of the leprous house and the events at the fall of Jericho, so too similar correspondences are to be detected between the laws relating to leprosy within people and the person of Rahab and her family. Here the connections are perhaps less prominent, suggesting that this is a subsidiary theme in the author's concerns, though nevertheless undoubtedly present.

To begin, we observe that according to the law of Lev 14, any person who enters, sleeps, or eats in the infected house is regarded as unclean (vv. 46–47). In such cases the uncleanness may be removed by a simple act of washing. Accepting that Jericho is being portrayed in the author's mind as a place diseased with leprosy, then into this category fall the two Hebrew spies who stayed overnight in the city. While the law includes those who "enter the house [והבא אל־הבית]," the Jericho narrative informs us (Josh 2:1) that the spies "entered the house [ויבאו בית]" of a woman in the city, a fact reiterated two verses later (v. 3, באו לביתך). If the analogy of the leprosy laws is applied, these men did not, so to speak, contract the disease, but did suffer from ritual uncleanness as a result, until they had undergone the washing in water. It is significant in this context that these two men, after leaving Jericho, are said to have crossed the Jordan (Josh 2:23)[6] before returning to the camp of Israel. Thus, in the narrative account, the ceremonial requirement has, in a sense, been satisfied.

With respect to Rahab and those residing in her house the situation is different. These were not merely temporary visitors to Jericho but native inhabitants. To the thinking of the author, therefore, these people were not merely rendered unclean by dwelling in the city but had equally contracted the same disease. Rahab was said to have been "living in the wall" (Josh 2:15), which according to Leviticus was a part of the house that was affected and needed treatment.

The levitical laws allow that in certain cases those suffering from leprosy could, by some unspecified means, be cured of the disease and their bodies restored to full health. In these instances a particular ritual of purification had to be enacted. This is described in some detail in Lev 14. There is reason to believe, through a number of allusions woven into his narrative, that the author of the book of Joshua saw Rahab, along with those in her household, in terms of a leper who had been cured of leprosy. It should be stressed that these are by nature only allusions to the practices performed in the case of leprosy. It is by no means intended that the rituals themselves were carried out wholly or in part, nor that the points of correspondence occur in the same order as found in the levitical text. Through the literary device of allusion, the author establishes connotation, which then in turn colors and enriches his narrative.

The central part of the purification ritual to be performed for the person in whom the infection has ceased is as follows:

> And the priest shall command that one of the birds be killed over fresh water in an earthen vessel. As for the living [החיה] bird, he shall take it, the cedar wood and the scarlet [שני] and the hyssop [האזב], and dip them and the living [החיה] bird in the blood of the bird killed over the fresh water. And he shall sprinkle it seven times on him who is to be cleansed from the leprosy, and shall pronounce him clean. (Lev 14:5–7)

Though the precise details regarding their use are lacking, scarlet and hyssop are essential components of the rite. The latter would have taken the form of a bunch of twigs from a particular plant which was especially employed in cleansing rituals. The former is described by

---

6. The verb ויעברו alone plainly denotes the crossing, or fording, of the river, as noted in Adolph Harstad, *Joshua* (CC; Saint Louis: Concordia, 2004), 145, "The implied direct object of this verb is the Jordan River, as is made clear by the use of this verb in 1:2, 14." Cf. also NIV, "forded the river" and NLT, "crossed the Jordan River."

modern translators as "scarlet string" (NASB) or "scarlet yarn" (NIV). According to rabbinic interpretations, this was tied to one of the birds, the one that was to be preserved alive.[7]

Here it is argued that this cleansing ritual is alluded to in the Jericho narratives in connection with Rahab, the woman who had assisted the Israelite spies. In return for the kindness that she had shown them, Rahab asked, "Give me a sign of good faith that you will preserve alive [והחיתם] my father and mother, my brothers and sisters, and all who belong to them" (Josh 2:12–13). The two men promise that this will be so (v. 14). When the city eventually falls, the promise is fulfilled, as Joshua declares, "Only Rahab the harlot shall live [תחיה], she and all who are with her in the house" (6:17; cf. v. 25, החיה). So this woman and her family are allowed to "live," and so in a way are comparable to the bird that is not slaughtered but kept alive.

In the narrative the distinguishing mark that sets Rahab and her family apart from the other inhabitants of Jericho is the cord of scarlet (השני) that she is directed to attach to the window of her house (Josh 2:18, 21). This corresponds to the piece of scarlet yarn which, according to a widely accepted interpretation, was attached to the bird that would remain alive. That such a conclusion is not stretching the imagination can be deduced from the parallels, noted in a previous article, between the deliverance of Rahab from Jericho and the deliverance of the Hebrews from Egypt in the exodus.[8] Whereas the one attaches a scarlet cord to the window, the other applies blood with hyssop to the doorposts (Exod 12:22). Hyssop is, of course, the other element, together with the blood, which forms a part of the cleansing ritual prescribed in Lev 14.[9] Blood also receives a mention in the Jericho account, where Rahab is warned,

---

7. Such an understanding is found, for example, in Maimonides's extensive treatment *On Leprosy*. Here he writes: "He [the priest] bound together the hyssop and the cedar; with the scarlet wool wound up lengthwise, and about them he put the tops of the wings and tips of the tail of the living bird, and dipped the four in the water and blood that were in the vessel" (cited in Henry Ainsworth, *Annotations on the Pentateuch and the Psalms*, vol. 1 [Edinburgh: Blackie & Sons, 1843], 551). Not all rabbinic sources accept this interpretation. Nevertheless, if not directly attached to the bird, there can be no doubt that the scarlet material and the bird are very closely associated in the ritual seeing that, according to Lev 14:6 itself, they are dipped into the blood of the slain bird simultaneously.

8. See Nicholas P. Lunn, "The Deliverance of Rahab (Joshua 2, 6) as the Gentile Exodus" *TynB* 65 (2014), 11–19.

9. Abraham ibn Ezra observes the connection between the purification of the leper and the Passover. See H. Norman Strickman and Arthur M. Silver, *Ibn Ezra's Commentary on the Pentateuch: Leviticus* (New York: Menorah, 2004), 105.

"If anyone goes out of the doors of your house into the street, his blood will be on his own head" (Josh 2:19), that is to say, that person will no longer be like the bird kept alive, but that whose blood is shed. The two parallel events, therefore, bring together the various components of the levitical rite.

Another probable allusion is the fact that Rahab and her family are initially placed "outside the camp [מחוץ למחנה] of Israel" (Josh 6:23). Here is a distinct echo of the leprosy laws where the one infected must remain "outside the camp [מחוץ למחנה]" for a specific period (Lev 13:46; 14:3). Following this Rahab and her kin are evidently permitted to "live in the midst of Israel" (Josh 6:25), just as the purified leper may come into the camp (Lev 14:8).

There is another possible, more distant and more curious, point of contact between Rahab and the leper as depicted in Leviticus. As an indication of their diseased condition the person afflicted with leprosy was obligated (Lev 13:45) to let the hair of his or her head to "be unkempt" (NIV) or "hang loose" (NLT). The Hebrew clause here וראשו יהיה פרוע, translated in the LXX as καὶ ἡ κεφαλὴ αὐτοῦ ἀκατακάλυπτος, literally means "and his head [will be] uncovered." What is significant about this is that such a state with regard to the hair is also that associated with an immoral woman. In the case of the suspected adulteress, part of the instruction for the priest is ופרע את־ראש האשה (Num 5:18), rendered as καὶ ἀποκαλύψει τὴν κεφαλὴν τῆς γυναικός, "and he will uncover the head of the woman."[10] In the Joshua narrative, of course, Rahab is identified as a זונה (Josh 2:1; 6:17, 25; LXX: πόρνη), which most naturally bears the meaning of "sexually immoral woman," whether a "prostitute" (see Gen 34:31; 38:15) or "adulteress" (see Hos 2:4; 3:1).[11] The hair, therefore, at least by implication, may establish a further point of contact at the conceptual level between the two texts—the leper and immoral women were both associated with the same particular condition of hair, whether dishevelled, loose, or exposed, according to how the terms are understood.

---

10. Behind the New Testament discussion of women covering their heads (1 Cor 11) there seems to be the same idea that woman with uncovered heads are indicating their immoral status. Note especially v. 5, "But every woman who prays or prophesies with her head uncovered [ἀκατακαλύπτῳ τῇ κεφαλῇ] dishonours her head," (cf. v. 13, and the similarity of language to the LXX renderings above).

11. In the New Testament Heb 11:31 and Jas 2:25 retain the usual understanding of this term. For a discussion of the Hebrew word זונה and the possible alternative meaning "innkeeper," see Harstad, *Joshua*, 108.

THE LEPROUS GARMENT

Lastly, and more briefly, we consider the third element of the leprosy law, which concerns the infection of various kinds of fabric, including wool, cotton, and leather (Lev 13:47–58). There is nothing in Josh 2 or 6 that appears to correspond with this. We do note, however, that Joshua commands the Israelites to refrain from taking various items from the city which are to be regarded as devoted to the Lord (Josh 6:19, 24). This sets the scene for what follows in the next chapter, in which the Israelites are evidently still located at Jericho (7:2). There we read that a Hebrew named Achan did in fact take certain things out of Jericho, contrary to the divine command (7:1). Later Achan admits that he had taken a garment from Shinar as well as amounts of silver and gold (v. 21).

Without doubt the first of the plundered items would be covered by the leprosy laws, since they state "When a garment has a mark of leprosy in it, whether it is a woollen garment or a linen garment, whether in warp or woof, of linen or of wool, whether in leather or in any article made of leather . . ." (Lev 13:47–48). Here we see both an analogy and a contrast with what has been earlier argued concerning the city and Rahab. Since the city is, by connotation, treated as a leprous house and broken down, and since Rahab and her family are regarded as lepers who undergo a manner of purification before being brought in among the people of Israel, it may reasonably be considered that the garment wrongfully taken by Achan falls under the category of a garment infected with the same disease. Yet in this case the outcome is different. Achan brings the infected item into his own tent, an act which has serious consequences for his own household and the whole of Israel, as chapter 7 makes apparent. Whereas Israel had brought about the downfall of a city of Canaan, an object removed from that city and brought into their camp leads to the defeat of Israel.[12]

According to the levitical law, an item of clothing that has become infected must be destroyed by fire. The prescription states that the officiating priest "shall burn the garment, whether the warp or the woof, in wool or in linen, or any article of leather which has the infection in it, for it is malignant leprosy; it shall be burned in the fire [באש תשרף]"

---

12. That the narrator is here intentionally creating a parallel between Rahab and Achan has been advocated in a convincing study by Frank Spina (*The Faith of the Outsider: Exclusion and Inclusion in the Biblical Story* [Grand Rapids, Eerdmans, 2005], 52–71). Among the more notable of the corresponding elements is the fact that Rahab "hid" the spies coming to Jericho (Josh 2:6) and was delivered, whereas Achan "hid" the items removed from Jericho (7:21, 22) and perished. In each instance the same Hebrew verb (טמן) is employed, establishing a clear link between the two.

(Lev 13:52). Only fire could, it would seem, remove the infection. It is surely no coincidence that this is the very same fate shared by Achan and his family, the burning of offenders then being an extremely rare practice in Israel. Joshua 7:25 tells us that once the plundered items were discovered, he was taken with his family "And all Israel stoned them with stones, and they burned them with fire [וישרפו . . . באש]." Achan and his household, therefore, having taken into his tent the forbidden items corresponding to the infected items of the leprosy law, has now contracted the same disease, so to speak, and so suffers the same fate as the leprous garment.[13]

Conclusion

The foregoing article has detected a number of allusions in the Jericho narratives to the levitical laws concerning leprosy. It is argued that this was a deliberate literary device on the part of the author. The purposeful nature is suggested by the fact that the allusions relate to three particular entities—a walled construction (house/city), a person (Rahab), and a garment (a garment of Shinar). These three, and these three exclusively, are treated in the leprosy laws of Lev 13–14. The deliberateness is further corroborated by the repetition of key words, phrases, and concepts in both contexts, in connection with all three of the foregoing entities.

In sum, through the subtle use of these allusions the writer of the book of Joshua is portraying the city of Jericho as a leprous house. It has been examined and warrants the dismantling specified by the levitical law. Though an inhabitant of the city, and therefore infected with the same disease, Rahab undergoes a manner of purification, no doubt by her faith in the God of Israel, and she and her family after a period of exclusion are joined to Israel. Conversely, Achan, an Israelite, removes forbidden items, including a special garment, from within the city and places them in his tent. Both he and his family may thus be viewed as contracting the same disease that had infected Jericho and Rahab before her cleansing. Achan and all that belongs to him suffers the burning by

---

13. There is a possible further link between Leviticus and the Achan incident. The term rendered as "malignant" in Lev 13:52 above is the Hebrew ממארת, which is of uncertain meaning. The fact is, however, that the rabbis traditionally associate it with the noun מארה, meaning "curse" (cf. Jacob Milgrom, *Leviticus 1–16: A New Translation with Introduction and Commentary* [AB3; New York: Doubleday, 1991], 811). In Josh 7, the term חרם also has connotations of something cursed, and is translated as such in the LXX (ἀνάθεμα) as well as some modern English versions (NKJV, "accursed things"; NJB, "under the curse of destruction"). Thus in the two texts there is the destruction by fire of that which is, in a manner, "cursed."

fire prescribed by Leviticus for the infected garment. The whole thus presents a consistency in the manner of allusion, which again argues for its purposeful design.[14]

The intention of the author through the means discussed can be plausibly surmised. In depicting Jericho, the first city of the promised land to be encountered, in this particular manner, the need is impressed upon the people of Israel for the wholesale eradication of the original occupants. They are seen as infected with a dangerous disease, one that is spiritual rather than physical. Implicit also is the severe warning, expressed through what happened to Achan, about contact with the Canaanites.[15] This is equally applicable to later generations of Israelites, when there still remained numerous Canaanite settlements among the twelve tribes, as much as to the generation of the conquest. Besides instruction and warning for Israel, the same allusions offer a degree of hope for the Canaanites themselves. While their utter destruction is divinely commanded, the possibility exists for cleansing, forsaking the practices of Canaan for the hope of Israel (cf. Josh 2:9–11), as illustrated through the deliverance of Rahab and her family.

---

14. Such an allusive form of reference as proposed here would be similar to the better known and oft-cited case concerning the Levite and his concubine found in Judg 19. Here the text contains distinct echoes of the Sodom narrative in Gen 19. The connotation established by means of this allusion is evidently that one of the towns of Israel, namely Gibeah, had lapsed into the same moral degradation as had been found in pagan Sodom. See, for example, Tammi J. Schneider, *Judges* (BO; Collegeville: Liturgical, 1999), 260–62.

15. It is of some interest to note that the three different kinds of objects taken by Achan—silver, gold, a garment—appear together in Gen 24:53 ("articles of silver and articles of gold, and garments") in a context having unmistakable marital overtones, where they appear to form all or part of the bride-price for Rebekah. By implication Achan, in receiving these same valuable items from Jericho is in a figure showing his willingness to enter into union with the inhabitants of the land.

A Remnant Will Return: An Analysis of the Literary Function of the Remnant Motif in Isaiah

ANDREW M. KING

The Southern Baptist Theological Seminary
aking@sbts.edu

The remnant motif has been rightly recognized as a significant feature in the Hebrew Bible. And yet, while various studies have helpfully catalogued its occurrences, far too little attention has been given to developing the motif as a complex literary device. This article assesses the nature of the remnant motif in the book of Isaiah. It is argued that the motif exhibits a two-fold function as both a threat of impending judgment as well as an indication of blessing. To accomplish this task, this article surveys the relevant passages under two primary categories: 1) the remnant motif in prophetic oracle and 2) the remnant motif in prophetic narrative. Within each of these sections, the motif is shown to have a positive or negative literary function. In prophetic oracles, the motif is used with both senses with respect to Judah yet only functions negatively when used in relation to the nations. The motif is used in Isaiah's prophetic narratives in order to further the negative and positive characterization of Ahaz and Hezekiah respectively. It is argued that a proper understanding of the dual nature of this motif benefits not only readers of the Hebrew Bible, but also aids proper interpretation of various New Testament passages.

KEYWORDS: *Remnant, Isaiah, Judgment, Ahaz, Hezekiah, Oracles Against the Nations*

The concept of remnant is unquestionably prominent in the Hebrew Bible. In some instances, only the presence of the motif itself can reconcile the tension between salvation and judgment.[1] Of its many instances

---

1. One clear example is the destruction decreed upon "all flesh" in Gen 6:13—the single exception of Noah and his family. See M. W. Elliott, "Remnant," in *New Dictionary of Biblical Theology* (ed. Brian S. Rosner et al. Downers Grove: InterVarsity, 2000), 723. Sirach 47:17 clearly understands Noah as a prototypical remnant community: "Noah was

in the Hebrew Bible, the Latter Prophets make regular use of remnant imagery, not least of which is found in the book of Isaiah. The sheer number of relevant lexical occurrences in the book evidence the significance of the motif as a literary feature. And while the positive aspects of the remnant in Isaiah are almost universally recognized, one neglected dimension is the use of the motif as a word of judgment itself. Here it functions not as evidence of YHWH's mercy and blessing but rather as a picture of the severity of judgment. While the former may not be completely absent, the emphasis falls on the negative aspect of the motif in the latter.

This article will argue that the remnant motif in Isaiah embodies two distinct literary functions in the book, both as a *threat* in contexts of judgment, as well as a *guarantee of hope* in contexts of salvation. The malleability of the motif enables this flexible usage in either context in the book.[2] As will be shown, the remnant pictures both how bad the situation in Judah is or will be (negative sense) and the purpose of YHWH to preserve and prosper his people (positive sense).

By way of procedure, this article will first survey the relevant passages regarding the remnant motif in the book of Isaiah, dividing the texts into two primary categories: 1) the remnant motif in prophetic oracles and 2) the remnant motif in prophetic narrative. While remnant theology could arguably be invoked in the wake of any scene of judgment in the book, the scope of this article will be confined to instances of the motif expressed by relevant lexical data, as well as explicit contextual indicators. Admittedly, the broad sweep of this survey precludes exhaustive analysis of each passage. These dual categories, however, will serve to explicate the two-fold literary function of the motif more broadly. Finally, in light of the conclusions drawn from the data, this article will briefly assess the significance of the motif for the theology of the New Testament.

---

found perfect and righteous; in the time of wrath he was taken in exchange; for this reason there was a remnant [κατάλειμμα] left on the earth when the flood came."

2. For the purposes of this analysis, the final form of the book is the locus of investigation. In other words, this article does not pursue the historical question of the diachronic development of the motif but rather focuses on the literary function in the canonical shape of the book. My reading of the motif is not dependent on a particular view of Isaianic authorship. For discussion on synchronic approaches to Isaiah, see Brevard S. Childs, *Introduction to the Old Testament as Scripture* (Philadelphia: Fortress, 1979), 325–34; Christopher R. Seitz, *Prophecy and Hermeneutics: Toward a New Introduction to the Prophets* (Studies in Theological Interpretation; Grand Rapids: Baker, 2007), 93–111. For a survey of contemporary approaches, see Jim McInnes, "A Methodological Reflection on Unified Readings of Isaiah," *Colloquium* 42 (2010): 67–84.

The Remnant Motif in Prophetic Oracles

This first category constitutes the most prominent setting for the motif in Isaiah. This section will survey oracles under three headings: 1) the remnant motif as threat against the nations; 2) the remnant motif as indication of blessing for Judah; and 3) the remnant motif as threat against Judah. It may be noted that there exists no instance of the remnant motif as an indication of blessing for the nations in Isaiah. If classified correctly, these texts evidence the two-fold function of the motif as both a positive and negative literary feature.

Remnant as a Threat against the Nations

Isaiah specifically employs the remnant motif in six texts in the Oracles against the Nations, portending the severity of the coming destruction (14:22, 30; 15:9; 16:14; 17:3; 24:6). The narrow scope of judgment, excluding only Assyria, Cush, and Egypt, expands to a global scale. With respect to the remnant, Isaiah never utilizes the motif positively in any of these occurrences.

Chapter 13 announces judgment on Babylon (13:1–22). This unit is followed by the denunciation of Babylon's king (14:4–23), with a salvation oracle concerning Israel situated in between (14:1–3). YHWH concludes his taunt with a decree to cut off from Babylon both "name and remnant (שְׁאָר), descendants and posterity" (14:22). The two pairs of coordinating phrases display the fruitless future of the nation, as the only hope of offspring is severed. The rhetorical effect of the language is clear: YHWH's judgment of Babylon is comprehensive. The great name the nation once enjoyed will be reduced to nothing more than a vague memory. In this context the remnant rhetorically depicts the severity of the impending destruction YHWH will accomplish.

The second oracle is announced against Philistia in 14:30. Set in the year that Ahaz died (v. 28), Isaiah prophesies the downfall of Philistia, establishing a contrast between the poor and needy who dwell in safety and those who will be killed by a divine famine (v. 30). More specifically, the disaster is said to fall upon the root (שֹׁרֶשׁ) and remnant (שְׁאֵרִית) of Philistia. The mention of "root" here may initially appear enigmatic, as one would expect a conceptually parallel noun to "remnant." Yet, the context of judgment may shed light on its usage here. The noun שֹׁרֶשׁ is found in several passages in the Latter Prophets to indicate the extent of destruction that will be accomplished (cf. Isa 5:24; Hos

9:16; Amos 2:9; Mal 4:1).[3] Though "root" and "remnant" are not conceptually equivalent, the parallelism indicates that both the source of Philistia's life ("root") and remaining population will be decimated.[4] Thus, the destruction of the Philistines will encompass the whole of the population, from young to old, first to last, with the remnant motif illustrating the universality of judgment.

The next two occurrences of the remnant motif in the Oracles against the Nations address Moab (15:9; 16:14). The unit begins with a lament of Moab's cities that have been laid waste (15:1–6). The desperate outcry of the nation had done little to secure safety and comfort for the people (v. 2). The sound of their wailing was audible even to the most distant regions of their territory (v. 8).[5] And though the land had been filled with the carnage of judgment, with rivers of blood reminiscent of the plagues of Egypt, YHWH would bring yet more (v. 9). Isaiah labels those who have survived the initial slaughter "escapees of Moab" (פליטת מואב) and the "remnant of the land" (שארית אדמה). The fate of these survivors, however was no brighter than that of those lining the bloody riverbanks. One like a lion was to come upon them (v. 9c). The image of the remnant here expresses the hopelessness of the nation, as judgment will be dealt fully and the remnant itself destroyed.

The second instance of the remnant motif as a threat against Moab comes at the close of the section (16:14). The wailing begun in 15:2 continues through the end of chapter 16, detailing the nation's demise. Isaiah concludes the unit by reaffirming the certainty of judgment within a chronological framework (v. 14). After three years, Moab, despite its glory and grandeur, would be brought to shame, leaving only a weak remnant (שאר) behind.

While the previous mention of the remnant in 15:9 is more forceful in its threatening character, the motif in 16:14 carries a subtler tone of despair. At the climax of the prediction of judgment, Isaiah marks a specific time in Moab's near future where it will be brought low. The

---

3. Wildberger understands the "root" mentioned in the previous verse (v. 29) to function epexegetically, with the meaning of father/predecessor. The two verses, then, would describe both the thoroughness of blessing (29c–30b) and the threat of judgment (29a, 30c–d). See H. Wildberger, *Isaiah 13–27: A Continental Commentary* (trans. T. H. Trapp Minneapolis: Fortress, 1997), 96.

4. So Gerhard F. Hasel, *The Remnant: The History and Theology of the Remnant Idea from Genesis to Isaiah* (2nd ed.; Andrews University Monographs 5; Berrien Springs, MI: Andrews University Press, 1974), 335; Wildberger, *Isaiah 13–27*, 97.

5. G. V. Smith, *Isaiah 1–39* (NAC 15A; Nashville: B & H, 2007), 331.

prophet need not recast the vision of bloodshed that will precede this remnant, but allows the silence of the empty land to portray the reality of desolation. Thus, to this point in the Oracles against the Nations this verse constitutes the most positive use of the motif. It is one, however, that is itself hardly a message of hope.[6]

The remnant motif further serves as a threat against Syria in 17:3 during the events of the Syro-Ephramite coalition. The chapter, beginning with a משא heading, identifies Damascus as the object of the oracle (v. 1).[7] The climax of 17:1–3 comes with the prediction of the parallel destinies of "children of Israel" and "the remnant of Aram" (שאר ארם). The reader can discern a note of irony as Israel's glory serves as the archetype of Syria's future standing. Verses 1–3 together present two empty kingdoms, void of fortresses, brought low in judgment.[8] The following verses (4–6) continue the negative imagery in terms of a malnourished man (v. 4) and a barren olive tree (v. 6). The remnant motif thus functions as a threat against both Syria and Ephraim in like fashion to the other nations addressed in the larger literary unit. Whereas the nation was established, the destruction executed by YHWH will reach even to the remnant.

The final occurrence of the remnant motif as a threat against the nations is found in the announcement of judgment in chapter 24. Following the Oracles against the Nations, Isaiah expands YHWH's

---

6. Hasel (*The Remnant*, 372) views the positive and negative aspects of the remnant motif as equally present in the passage.

7. A problem arises in verse 2 with the mention of Aroer (ערער) as a seeming parallel capital city alongside Damascus. The Hebrew Bible includes 15 references to cities called Aroer, but none of which lay in close proximity to Syria. There have been four primary solutions offered in response: 1) identify an otherwise unknown city in Syria as the referent here (John Oswalt, *The Book of Isaiah*, vol. 1 [NICOT; Grand Rapids: Eerdmans, 1986], 348); 2) treat verse two as a misplaced editorial insertion (Wildberger, *Isaiah 13–27*, 168); 3) view the text as corrupted needing emendation (following the LXX); 4) view the Aroer here as an Israelite city (Joseph Blenkinsopp, *Isaiah 1–39: A New Translation with Introduction and Commentary* [AB; New York: Doubleday, 2000], 304). Though this text presents difficulty, the need for emendation is unwarranted with the MT as perfectly intelligible in the literary framework of the passage. It is best to see the Aroer mentioned here as the city located in the territory previously allotted to Reuben (Deut 2:36; Josh 12:2; 2 Kgs 10:33), which itself later fell under the dominion of Syria. With an ABBA pattern linking the downfall of Syria (A) to that of Israel (B), the interconnectedness of the unit precludes the need for emendation or the relocation of the passage. So J. A. Motyer, *The Prophecy of Isaiah: An Introduction & Commentary* (Downers Grove: InterVarsity, 1993), 156.

8. Contra Motyer (*The Prophecy of Isaiah*, 156–57), who takes the remnant here as another instance of Gentile inclusion.

desolation to the whole earth as those who have violated the everlasting covenant.[9] The world is consumed by a curse that dispenses the retributive justice of YHWH as the penalty for its guilt. In the wake of YHWH's justice only a few (שְׁאָר) are left alive (24:6). The circumstances out of which the remnant appears evince its literary function in illustrating the negative connotation of the motif. Here again, the remnant displays how bad the situation is in the wake of judgment. In the final analysis, the remnant motif, as surveyed in this study, serves only as a threat when used in reference to the nations. Among the images of desolation employed by Isaiah, the remnant motif serves as an apt illustration of the severity of YHWH's judgment.

Remnant as an Indication of Blessing for Judah

In contrast to the threat of judgment, Isaiah presents five instances of the remnant motif in contexts of blessing for Judah (4:3; 10:20–21; 11:11, 16; 28:5; 46:3–4). Together, these passages emphasize both the temporal and future realities of salvation for those who are faithful to YHWH. What remains after judgment is a purified community who, being led through a new exodus, experiences the blessing and protection of YHWH.[10] Of these five passages, four occur as a positive feature of the Day of YHWH.[11]

---

9. Though it may be argued that the "everlasting covenant" here is a reference to the covenant made with Noah in Gen 9:16, various factors stand against this interpretation. One obstacle for this view is the mention of transgression/violation of the laws and statutes. Such covenant obligations were not applicable to those outside Israel, and thus the scope of this covenant should be kept within the borders of the covenant people. Paul R. Raabe rightly notes the prophetic tendency to employ rhetorical of universal judgment for specific exhortations in a local situations, here being the sin of Israel. See Paul R. Raabe, "The Particularizing of Universal Judgment in Prophetic Discourse," *CBQ* 64 (2002): 652–74. I am particularly indebted to Duane A. Garrett for his interaction on this passage.

10. Webb states that the purification of Zion is the key to its transformation, a fact that holds the key to the structure of Isaiah as a whole. See Barry G. Webb, "Zion in Transformation: A Literary Approach to Isaiah," in *Bible in Three Dimensions: Essays in Celebration of Forty Years of Biblical Study* (ed. David J. A. Clines, Stephen E. Fowl, and Stanley E. Porter; JSOTSup 87; Sheffield: Sheffield Academic Press, 1990).

11. Many view the Day of YHWH as a central concern of the Latter Prophets. VanGemeren identifies six features of the Day of YHWH in the Hebrew Bible: 1) the Day signifies YHWH's intrusion into human affairs; 2) the Day brings judgment on all creation; 3) the Day is historical and eschatological; 4) on the Day, all creation will submit to YHWH's sovereignty, willingly or not; 5) no social distinction is observed on that Day, but rather, the righteous are separated from the wicked; and 6) the Day signifies

The first text is Isa 4:2–6, which, following the judgment of 3:1–4:1, describes a purified people who are led through a new exodus, constituting a holy remnant. The ביום ההוא formula at the beginning of verse 2 links the events of chapter 4 with the eschatological destruction foretold in the previous chapter. The section (4:2–6) opens with a description of the beautiful and glorious landscape of the renewed Jerusalem (v. 2).[12] Isaiah describes the remnant community both as those who are "left [יתר] in Zion" and those who "remain [שאר] in Jerusalem" (4:3). It is clear that this remnant has survived the devastation of YHWH's judgment. But more than merely continuing a meager existence, these survivors emerge as a holy people (vv. 3–4). The purpose of YHWH is to cleanse those in Jerusalem by judgment, establishing a new, faithful wilderness generation.[13] As a clear statement about the positive

---

vindication, glorification, and full redemption of the godly. See Willem, VanGemeren, *Interpreting the Prophetic Word: An Introduction to the Prophetic Literature of the Old Testament* (Grand Rapids: Zondervan, 1996), 174–76; Greg A. King, "The Day of the Lord in Zephaniah," *BibSac* 152 (1995): 16–32; Rolf Rendtorff, "Alas for the Day!: The 'Day of the Lord' in the Book of the Twelve," in *God in the Fray: A Tribute to Walter Brueggemann* (ed. Tod Linafelt and Timothy K. Beal; Minneapolis: Fortress, 1998), 186–197; Paul R. House, "The Day of the Lord," in *Central Themes in Biblical Theology: Mapping Unity in Diversity* (ed. Scott J. Hafemann and Paul R. House; Grand Rapids: Baker, 2007), 179–224.

12. A considerable amount of debate has emerged regarding the proper interpretation of the branch of YHWH (צמח יהוה), with a common view of the branch as representative of the messianic king described elsewhere in the Hebrew Bible. Yet, such a reading does not make the best sense of the context, especially in relation to the parallel subject "the fruit of the land." The construction itself (צמח יהוה) occurs only here in the Hebrew Bible. This is not to say that Isaiah (cf. 11:1), among other authors (cf. Jer 23:5), could not use the term messianically, but to require a messianic interpretation based solely on lexical grounds may demand too much of the lexeme. Rather, the branch here describes the new habitation of the glorified remnant, which itself is a drastic reversal of the unfortunate conditions previously experienced by the nation. Whereas YHWH had formerly cut off the sustaining resources of Jerusalem and Judah (3:1), he now personally restores the fortunes of the "survivors of Israel." For support of this interpretation, see Hasel, *The Remnant*, 263; Otto Kaiser, *Isaiah 1–12: A Commentary* (trans. R. A. Wilson; OTL; Philadelphia: Westminster, 1972), 1:54; Blenkinsopp, *Isaiah 1–39*, 203; John D. W. Watts, *Isaiah 1–33* (WBC 24; Dallas: Word, 1985), 49. The LXX deviates significantly from the MT with the reading ἐπιλάμψει ὁ θεὸς ἐν βουλῇ ἦμετ ἀδόξης ἐπ ἰτῆς γῆς. Such a translation could have risen from the understanding of an Aramaic verbal form of צמח ("to shine"). See Rodrigo Franklin De Sousa, *Eschatology and Messianism in LXX Isaiah 1–12* (LHBOTS 516; New York: T&T Clark, 2010), 64.

13. This link to Israel's previous history is seen in verse 5 as the imagery of the cloud by day and fire by night brings to remembrance YHWH's deliverance of Israel from Egypt (Exod 13:21–22). This inner-biblical allusion serves to show that the covenant relationship enjoyed by ancient Israel will be appropriated to the eschatological remnant community. So Hasel, *The Remnant*, 266.

future of the remnant community, Isa 4:2–6 establishes a hope beyond the destruction of the Day of YHWH for those who remain.

A second occurrence of the remnant motif as an indication of blessing for Judah is found in Isa 10. Here a negative use of the remnant motif (10:22–23), discussed below, forms a sharp contrast to the hopeful description of the remnant's future (10:20–21).[14] Here, standing in parallel to "survivors [פליטת] of the house of Jacob" (v. 20), the remnant is said to alter its allegiance from Assyria to YHWH.[15] The positive aspect of the remnant is substantiated by the parallel phrase, with the root פלט being used only of Israel in a positive sense in Isaiah (4:2; 37:31–32). Those who survive the judgment of YHWH in the text are renewed in their trust, returning to their mighty God. The phrase שאר ישוב ("a remnant will return") (v. 21a) constitutes the second occurrence of this expression in the book (cf. 7:3), clearly indicating a positive situation for Judah. Rather than returning to a geographical location, Judah will return to a person, namely YHWH. With this restoration, the positive sense of the phrase cannot be missed. Having established the positive aspect of the remnant in verses 20–21, these comments will suffice for the present section, though a further analysis of these verses will be resumed below.

A third instance of the remnant as blessing for Judah is found in chapter 11. Isaiah, following a description of the righteous reign of a messianic figure (vv. 1–10), links the renewed conditions of the earth to the ingathering of the remnant community who have been scattered across the world. A ביום ההוא formula connects verse 11 with its parallel in verse 10, where the Davidic messiah is described as a counselor for the nations. At that time, YHWH declares his intention to purchase for a second time the "remnant that remains of his people" (שאר עמו אשר ישאר) dwelling in foreign lands (v. 11). This miraculous deliverance is a new

---

14. The sudden shift in tone leads many scholars to label the passage as secondary (cf. Hans Wildberger, *Isaiah 1–12: A Commentary* [trans. Thomas H. Trapp; Minneapolis: Fortress, 1991], 435). Yet, the dual sense of the remnant motif allows this passage to be read as a unity at the literary level.

15. Many have noted the historical problem raised by this passage, particularly in relation to the events in the time of Ahaz. The discussion typically centers on the fact that though Ahaz did rely on Assyria, he was not struck by the nation (2 Kgs 16). Some scholars have argued for a delayed fulfillment in the time of Hezekiah in an effort to alleviate the tension. Oswalt is likely correct stating the passage does not specify a particular nation, but represents any nation that would contend with YHWH for Israel's trust. The eschatological character of the passage lends further support to this conclusion. See Bernhard Duhm, *Das Buch Jesaia* (5th ed.; Göttingen: Vandenhoeck & Ruprecht, 1902), 75; Kaiser, *Isaiah 1–12*, 147; Hasel, *The Remnant*, 322–23; Oswalt, *The Book of Isaiah*, vol. 1, 270.

exodus.[16] With the previous mention of the righteous reign of the messiah, the remnant, presumably, will be led to the new promised land where the Davidic messiah will be enthroned.[17] Yet, like the first exodus, the remnant will not depart before plundering (בזז) the nations where they were in exile (11:14; cf. Exod 3:22). Moreover, the new exodus not only serves to free the remnant from her captivity, but also brings peace between the northern and southern kingdoms (11:13). Moreover, the result of YHWH's action creates a direct route from the nations to the land of Israel in order to speed their return. So Isaiah, for a second time, utilizes the exodus from Israel's early history as a pattern of deliverance for the remnant community in the future.[18]

The next instance of the remnant motif used as an indication of blessing for Judah occurs in 28:5. Opening with an oracle against the leaders of the northern kingdom, Isaiah portrays them in terms of a drunkard lacking sober judgment. Verse 5 begins with another ביום ההוא statement, alluding to the judgment previously mentioned against Israel.[19] By use of parallel language and imagery, a contrast is clearly established between the future blessing of the remnant community and an indictment against Ephraim. Samaria, the capital city of the northern kingdom, is addressed as a "crown of pride" adorning the senseless nation. Yet the beauty of the city is already fading like a wilting flower

---

16. While the mention of a second redemption in Isa 11:11 has provoked much scholarly debate, the imagery in the passage evokes once again the exodus from Egypt as its reference point. A combination of features in the text bears out this conclusion, the first of which is the mention of Egypt itself (vv. 11, 15, 16). Second, the following description of a miraculous deliverance from foreign lands, particularly in verse 15, further supports the thematic connection, as Israelites who have been banished and dispersed to alien regions will once again walk through river channels on land that YHWH has dried up (cf. Exod 14:21–22). As with many other biblical authors, Isaiah presents the exodus as a paradigmatic model for YHWH's future deliverance of the remnant. For the literary function of appeals to ancient traditions, see Norman C. Habel, "Appeal to Ancient Tradition as a Literary Form," *ZAW* 88 (1976): 253–72.

17. Smith, *Isaiah 1–39*, 276. Watts (*Isaiah 1–33*, 179) correctly views the mention of the nations as anticipating the "four corners of the earth" in verse 12.

18. Here, the character quality of the remnant is evident in the following chapter (Isa 12). The remnant proclaims the salvation of their God who has turned his away his anger. Such a declaration is a fitting conclusion to the literary unit of Isa 1–11, as YHWH is said to dwell in the midst of his purified people (12:6). See Webb, "Zion in Transformation," 73.

19. The sudden shift in verses 5 and 6 to a positive note of prosperity appear seemingly as an interruption of the diatribe against Ephraim resumed again in verse 7. Yet at this point in the book such contrasting tones may not be unexpected (cf. 10:20–24 below).

(v. 1, 4).[20] In characteristic response to the proud, YHWH acts to bring low the arrogance of the people, readying one, generally acknowledged as Assyria, to bring swift destruction (vv. 2–4). This devastation is juxtaposed to the blessing of the remnant community (שאר) who is decked not with a "crown of pride" but rather with YHWH as a "crown of glory" (v. 5).[21] Isaiah furthers the contrast with a masterful word play in verses 4–5: whereas Samaria, situated at the head (ראש) of the lush valley (v. 4), was soon to be destroyed, the remnant (שאר), adorned with YHWH's presence, will dwell in security. The reversal of the consonants of ראש and שאר displays the inverse fates of each respective group.[22]

The final instance of the remnant motif as an indication of blessing for Judah comes in the contrast drawn between the idols of Babylon and YHWH in chapter 46. While the gods of Babylon do nothing more than burden those who carry them (v. 1–2), YHWH as the living God has borne "all the remnant [שארית] of the house of Israel" from their birth (v. 3).[23] In showing the futility of trusting in idols, YHWH summons all the people to hear and remember his work of

---

20. The referent of עטרת גאות, whether the leaders of the nation or its capital city, is not clear in the Hebrew text. Several indications, however, support Samaria as the preferable option. First, that the leaders are envisioned as the drunkards themselves is clarified by verses 7 and 14, which, directly addressing national leaders, continue the pattern of verse 1. If correct, the crown here would require a different referent then the leaders. Second, a parallel phrase (עטרת תפארת) is used to later describe the city of Zion in 62:3. Finally, the location of the crown in the lush valley (1c) fits well with the geographical situation of Samaria. Though the crown metaphor can indeed represent individuals (cf. v. 5), these points support Samaria as the referent here. As such, the city of Samaria serves as the pinnacle of pride for the senseless leaders of the northern kingdom.

21. Some scholars, such as Motyer, have argued for a messianic interpretation of this passage, following the Targum. Yet the emphasis of the passage focuses on the direct relation of YHWH to remnant community. There does not seem to be indication of the inclusion of a messianic figure as an intermediary here. See Smith, *Isaiah 1–39*, 478; *pace* Motyer, *The Prophecy of Isaiah*, 44.

22. J. Cheryl Exum, "'Whom Will He Teach Knowledge?' A Literary Approach to Isaiah 28," in *Art and Meaning: Rhetoric in Biblical Literature* (ed. Alan J. Hauser, David J. A. Clines, and David M. Gunn; JSOTSup 19; Sheffield: JSOT Press, 1982), 117.

23. The remnant in 46:3b stands in parallel to "house of Jacob" in 3a, representing the whole of the people. Oswalt argues that the two lines form a case of stepped synonymous parallelism with both parts referring to the whole nation. See John Oswalt, *The Book of Isaiah*, vol. 2 (NICOT; Grand Rapids: Eerdmans, 1986), 226. Against this view is Delitzsch, who views the lines as differentiating the northern and southern kingdoms. See Franz Delitzsch, *Isaiah* (trans. James Martin Grand Rapids: Eerdmans, 1950), 2:233. Blenkinsopp (*Isaiah 40–55*, 268) rejects an identification of the northern kingdom in the verse, for whom the author of 40–55 supposedly "[manifests] no great interest."

redemption. The preservation of his covenant people, manifest in the remnant, is an act that no god of Babylon could accomplish. In comparison to the idols, YHWH is one who is able to keep his people, no matter how small, throughout the whole of their lives. And though the addressees would later be called "transgressors" (v. 8) and "stubborn of heart" (v. 12), verses 3–4 magnify the care of YHWH for the people, establishing a positive literary function for the remnant.[24]

As seen in this section, Isaiah makes use of the remnant motif to describe the blessing of YHWH towards his covenant people. The emphasis of the motif is one of hope, as YHWH prospers the nation, leading them through a new exodus. Yet unlike the previous wilderness generation, the remnant is marked by purity and faithfulness, standing opposite those who will be destroyed.

Remnant as an Indication of the Severity of Judgment on Judah

The final category for the remnant in prophetic oracles in the book of Isaiah is as an indication of the severity of judgment for Judah. Herein lies the most neglected, and perhaps most controversial, aspect of the remnant motif in contemporary discussion. While the motif itself can function as an illustration of the mercy and blessing of YHWH toward his covenant people, this secondary literary function portrays the extent and severity of destruction. In these texts, the author uses the concept of remnant as a polemic against unfaithful Judah in like fashion to the nations, describing the degree of desolation that will indeed occur. What is emphasized by the motif in these texts is not a future community that is plentiful and holy but rather a meager population left in the wake of YHWH's justice. As with the positive oracles of salvation, the negative oracles against Judah contain both a temporal, as well as eschatological, dimension. Isaiah utilizes the remnant motif in this way in three texts (1:9; 6:13; 10:22).

The first of these references comes in the opening chapter of the book, which details the coming devastation as a result of the nation's sin. Here, Isaiah describes the land as desolate and overthrown by foreigners (v. 7) with three pictures of its empty condition (v. 8): a booth in a vineyard, a hut in a cucumber field, and a besieged city. Together, these

---

24. So Klaus Baltzer (*Deutero-Isaiah: A Commentary on Isaiah 40–55* [trans. Margaret Kohl; Hermeneia; Minneapolis: Fortress, 2001], 258), though one need not agree with his view of the historical development of the motif. It should also be noted that a positive use of the remnant here does not preclude a future winnowing of the people. Precisely because of the mention of the infidelity of the nation in v. 8 and v. 12, one may expect such a future act of YHWH.

images show the devastating aftermath of an army that has executed the judgment of YHWH. In verse 9, Isaiah states, "If YHWH of hosts had not left [יתר] us a few survivors [שׂריד כמעט], we would be as Sodom, and be like Gomorrah."[25] The term "survivors" here is a label expressing the meager condition of the remnant.[26] While the mercy of YHWH can be seen in the sparing of a remnant,[27] the extent of the destruction seems to be the primary function of the motif in the passage.[28] In other words, the devastation would be so complete that if YHWH had not left these individuals in the land, the nation would be eradicated. The rhetoric in the passage demonstrates the gravity of the situation for Judah.[29]

A second instance of the remnant in the context of judgment is found in what has been traditionally understood as Isaiah's commission in 6:13. After receiving instruction to deaden the sensitivities of the people by his prophetic message, Isaiah cries out in despair, "How long, O YHWH?" (v. 11). The response hardly comforts the prophet, as YHWH conveys his intent to empty the cities of the land in judgment. As noted by every commentator on this passage, there exists a series of notoriously difficult text-critical and translation issues in this passage.[30] Though an exhaustive analysis is beyond the scope of the present article, I will attempt to frame an understanding of the passage focusing on the remnant motif. Though there is no explicit remnant *terminology* in this verse, justification for the its inclusion here will be provided below.

---

25. The adjective מעט is missing from LXX, Syriac, and Vulgate, leading some contemporary scholars to excise it from the text. On a literary level, however, there appears no compelling reason for this decision. So Wildberger, *Isaiah 1–12*, 20; Hasel, *The Remnant*, 314.

26. The LXX translates שׂריד as σπέρμα, possibly due to the influence of a similar phrase in Deuteronomy 3:3. The lexeme שׂריד frequently has a positive function in the Latter Prophets, yet here is used negatively in context. See Hasel, *The Remnant*, 314–15.

27. Motyer, *The Prophecy of Isaiah*, 44; Kaiser, *Isaiah 1–12*, 10.

28. Contra Childs, *Isaiah*, 19.

29. This interpretation is supported further by the character quality of the remnant itself visible from the following verse (v. 10). Isaiah transitions from a description of judgment to directly address the leaders of the very remnant that was spared, calling them "chiefs of Sodom." In this fashion, Isaiah states that though the remnant had not suffered the fate of Sodom and Gomorrah in total destruction, their character and practices are no less abominable (v. 13). With such a picture of the remnant community, one can hardly miss the negative literary function of the motif in the opening chapter.

30. For a concise summary and evaluation, see Jan de Waard, *A Handbook on Isaiah* (Textual Criticism and the Translator; Winona Lake, IN: Eisenbrauns, 1997), 1:29–31.

The first line of the passage, ועוד בה עשיריה, is generally translated as a conditional clause ("And if there is still a tenth in it"),[31] followed by the more difficult ושבה והיתה לבער. This latter phrase, translated "and it will again be consumed," utilizes שוב as an auxiliary verb, expressing the manner of action described by the final two words.[32] The translation of בער historically has proved problematic for commentators. The usual sense of the word, "to burn," does not appear to make the best sense of the context, as no fire is mentioned or implied. Some have aligned their translation with various ancient versions, such as Symmachus's "for grazing" (εις καταβοσκησιν),[33] but the rendering here of "consumed" better fits the present context, functioning similarly to the verb in 3:14.[34]

Together, these two lines describe a group remaining after an enemy attack, yet those who survive do so only to be consumed by more violence. The remnant concept implicit here would seem to indicate a remnant destined for future destruction. If the translation adopted here is correct, the negative implications of the motif cannot be missed. As Clements aptly states, "In spite of the textual difficulties, and the lack of a completely satisfactory resolution of them, it is evident that the metaphor is one expressing threat."[35]

Greg Beale, sharing this conclusion, argues for a negative understanding of the remnant motif, as itself an indictment of idolatry.[36] Anticipating objections regarding the "holy seed" of v. 13e, Beale

---

31. J. A. Emerton, "The Translation and Interpretation of Isaiah vi. 13," in *Interpreting the Hebrew Bible: Essays in Honour of E. I. J. Rosenthal* (ed. J. A. Emerton and S. C. Reif; Cambridge: Cambridge University Press, 1982), 86. Hasel (*The Remnant*, 239) states, "In Isaiah, however, the idea of the tenth contains no positive aspect. It has the character of a threat."

32. Gregory K. Beale, "Isaiah 6:9–13: A Retributive Taunt Against Idolatry," *VT* 41 (1991): 259; Emerton, "The Translation and Interpretation of Isaiah Vi. 13," 86. Emerton rejects the interpretation of שבה as indicative of some form of repentance, functioning rather as a complementary unit. See Ibid., 115.

33. So Wildberger, *Isaiah 1–12*, 251. The Vulgate's reading of "make plain" is likely based on the reading באר rather than בער.

34. Hasel, *The Remnant*, 235. Watts views the first two clauses (13a–b) as continuing the speech of the prophet, with a switch to YHWH as speaker in the third. He renders 13a–b as a questions: "if (perchance there be) yet in it a tenth-part, if it turn, will it be for burning?" (Watts, *Isaiah 1–33*, 68).

35. Clements, *Isaiah 1–39*, 78.

36. More specifically, Beale states that the idolatry of Israel functions as a "metonymy representing the whole of the nation's covenantal disobedience" (Beale, "Isaiah 6:9–13," 257).

presents a series of alternatives to a positive reading of this text. He notes that the ordinary use of the term מצבת represents a pillar, whether cultic or commemorative, making the common translation of "stump" unlikely.[37] What Isaiah is told, according to Beale, is that idolatrous Israel will be made deaf and dumb like their objects of worship. Those who remain will resemble their idols. Thus, destruction is the only fate for such a people. Beale concludes, "Therefore, Isaiah uses the remnant idea in both *v.* 13a and *v.* 13b not positively but negatively in order to emphasize the magnitude and absoluteness of Israel's judgment."[38]

Though I am not persuaded by some of Beale's broader conclusions on this text, he rightly understands the negative use of the remnant motif. Yet even if Beale's analysis is rejected, at the very least a contrast would be established between the remnant as an indication of judgment (v. 13a–b) and one of hope (v. 13e). In either case v. 13a–b would present the remnant motif as a negative literary feature.

The final use of the remnant motif as a negative literary feature is Isa 10:22. Framed by another formula ביום ההוא (v. 20), what begins as a positive use of the remnant motif as blessing for Judah (vv. 20–21) is suddenly darkened by the grave declaration of ruin. With an almost seamless transition from an allusion to the blessing of the Abrahamic covenant, Isaiah decrees devastation for Israel with only a remnant (שאר) remaining.[39] Together, these verses exhibit an A-B-A-B pattern.

A: a small, faithful remnant trusts YHWH (v. 20)

B: a positive use of the remnant—the people's future is secure in YHWH (v. 21)

---

37. Ibid., 268. Contra Dale W. Manor, "Massebah," in *Anchor Bible Dictionary* (ed. David Noel Freedman; New York: Doubleday, 1992). The phrase itself is omitted from LXX and the Old Latin, causing some to label it a later gloss. Emerton, who is among those who reject the phrase's originality, views a similar phrase in Ezra 9:2 as an indication of a post-exilic setting for the gloss. Yet Hasel has effectively argued how the phrase's occurrence in 1QIsa[a] attests to its antiquity. See Emerton, "The Translation and Interpretation of Isaiah vi. 13," 114; Hasel, *The Remnant*, 237.

38. Beale, "Isaiah 6:9–13," 271.

39. The כי אם construction at the beginning of verse 22 functions to introduce a concessive clause, contrasting the large number of Israelites at present with the small remnant that will return in the future. A conditional sense is syntactically possible for the construction, as in the confirmation of an oath, but the negative context of the oracle stands against this reading. Contra Motyer, *The Prophecy of Isaiah*, 117. See Christo H. J. van der Merwe, Jackie A. Naudé, and Jan H. Kroeze, *A Biblical Hebrew Reference Grammar* (Sheffield: Sheffield Academic Press, 1999), §40.5.2.

A': a large, (presumably unfaithful) remnant (v. 22a)

B': a negative use of the remnant—destruction lays hold of the majority of the people with only a meager remnant remaining (v. 22b)

The oscillation between salvation and judgment here may have a specific literary purpose, namely, to prevent any misunderstanding of YHWH's promise of prosperity.[40] Here, the remnant motif functions to warn against an unwarranted breed of nationalism. Isaiah makes clear that mere inclusion in the people of Israel is not an unconditional guarantee of safety, but faith and obedience are required. Thus, the progression of thought in 10:22 moves from promise to a sober reality of judgment for those who forsake YHWH while trusting unequivocally in their identity as members of the covenant.[41]

If the above analysis is correct, these three texts present the remnant motif as an indication of the judgment that will meet Judah. The motif provides an apt picture of the small population left after destruction, in some cases destined for further harm. While the presence of the remnant may imply the merciful character of YHWH in some of these verses, the primary literary function appears to depict the near hopelessness of those left alive. The moral character of the remnant, in some contexts, clarifies the warrant for this divine retribution. Only the most vivid of pictures could communicate the severity of Judah's situation, and for Isaiah, the remnant motif is well suited for this task.

THE REMNANT MOTIF IN PROPHETIC NARRATIVE

The second category of the remnant motif is found in the two prophetic narrative units (7:1–25; 36:1–37:38). Here, the literary function of the remnant reveals the prophetic perspective of Israel's leadership, contrasting the reigns of Ahaz and Hezekiah as negative and positive examples of kingship respectively.

---

40. So Hasel, *The Remnant*, 329.

41. Oswalt (*Book of Isaiah*, 1:271) rejects any abrogation of the Abrahamic covenant but states that the passage is a warning against trusting in one's identity as an Israelite. Though the mention of the remnant shows again the mercy of YHWH in sparing some of the people, the primary focus appears to be on the destruction that will occur. Contra Graham, "The Remnant Motif in Isaiah," 223.

The parallels between the two sections themselves can hardly be missed.[42] Both narratives, set in the context of the threat of invasion by foreign armies, occur in the same location—"the conduit of the upper pool on the highway to the Washer's Field" (7:3; 36:2). This location is referenced only in these two narratives and in the parallel account of chapter 36 in 2 Kgs 18. Furthermore, the progression of events establishes an obvious parallel as the report of the mounting threat provokes great anxiety in both kings, followed by signs of reassurance and the command of YHWH not to fear mediated through the prophet Isaiah. That the two literary units were intended to in some way parallel one another is clear, yet, the dissimilarities form an equally significant relationship.

While both narratives follow the same order of events, moving from crisis to promise, promise to sign, sign to response, the details in each narrative are in tension. Whereas in chapter 7 YHWH sends the prophet Isaiah to speak words of *comfort* to King Ahaz near the Washer's field in response to the military threat, the contrasting narrative (36–37) describes the king of Assyria sending his emissary, the Rabshakeh, to speak words of *threat* at the Washer's field. Furthermore, Ahaz's unbelief in rejecting the request for a sign (7:12) is contrasted with the silence of doubt in the Hezekiah narrative.[43] Together, the narratives present two models of leadership in Judah: one that rejects the covenant promises of YHWH and one that exhibits trust in the God of Israel. It is in the context of this contrast that the literary function of the remnant motif emerges.

Isaiah 7:3, 21

The remnant motif makes a two-fold appearance in chapter 7, both following the report of the coalition of Syria and the northern kingdom of Israel—an event that causes both the king and the nation of Judah to tremble like trees in the wind (v. 2). In response, the prophet Isaiah is instructed to assure the king that YHWH will indeed deliver the people by the use of a foreign military power. Almost in passing, Isaiah is

---

42. These observations are succinctly summarized in Edgar W. Conrad, "The Royal Narratives and the Structure of the Book of Isaiah," *JSOT* 41 (1988): 68–70.

43. The contrasting characterization of Ahaz and Hezekiah is heightened by Isaiah's omission of Hezekiah's attempt to financially appease Sennacherib recorded in 2 Kgs 18:14–16. The result is a more positive portrayal of Hezekiah in this instance over against that of Ahaz. So P. R. Ackroyd, *Isaiah 36–39: Structure and Function* (SBTS 5; Winona Lake: Eisenbrauns, 1995), 493.

commanded to take along his son, שְׁאָר יָשׁוּב ("a remnant will return") (v. 3). This constitutes the first reference to Isaiah's family in the book, who, as becomes clear later, prove to be significant in the prophet's own ministry as signs for Israel (cf. 8:18).

While clearly Isaiah's son contributes to the remnant theology of the book, the specific meaning of his name has posed some difficulty for interpreters.[44] Does the mention of a remnant reinforce the message of comfort to the king that a remnant will indeed return despite the threat to national security? Does the name imply the weight of a coming judgment, namely, that *only* a remnant will return after a devastating defeat? Or does the name pertain not to Israel itself but indicate that the enemy forces will be greatly diminished if they continue their advance? The immediate context of the passage provides no explicit answer to these questions. To complicate matters further, both the positive and negative use are found in proximity to this passage. In the case of 10:20–23, as argued above, both literary functions occur.

Yet, when set in the wider literary context, as well as in contrast to the Hezekiah narrative, the function of the name is clarified. It must be remembered that at this point in the literary world of chapter 7, Isaiah's son was a young boy, indicating that his name did not originate in direct response to the Syro-Ephramite threat.[45] Furthermore, the prediction of a remnant during the time of peace prior to this event would have no functional positive connotation, unless destruction was already anticipated. Thus on a literary level, the mention of the remnant at the beginning of the narrative casts a negative light on the chapter, as it anticipates Ahaz's rejection of YHWH's assurance.[46]

---

44. There have been various attempts to emend or offer alternative translations for the phrase, most of which have not gained a significant following. Though Roland de Vaux rightly appreciates the antiquity of remnant terminology, he incorrectly concludes that its meaning is self-evident, needing no explanation. See Roland de Vaux, *The Bible and the Ancient Near East* (Garden City, NY: Doubleday, 1971), 19. As argued here, there could be either a positive or negative sense intended in his name. For a defense of the traditional rendering of this phrase, see Gerhard F. Hasel, "Linguistic Considerations Regarding the Translation of Isaiah's Shear-Jashub: A Reassessment," *AUSS* 9 (1971): 36–46.

45. See the thesis by Johan M. Lundberg "Refugees, Survivors and a Community Saved and Refashioned through Judgement: The Remnant in Isaiah, Micah and Zephaniah," (M.A. thesis, MF Norwegian School of Theology, 2011, 18). Oswalt places the events of chapter 7 subsequent to Ahaz's defeat by the Syro-Ephramite league. What Ahaz now dreads, according to Oswalt, is total annihilation. Yet, this conclusion is not apparent to me in the text. See Oswalt, *The Book of Isaiah*, 1:200.

46. While it is true that verse 10 indicates a new unit in the literary progression of the chapter, it must not be separated from the preceding verses. In fact, the intelligibility of

The second mention of the remnant in Isa 7 occurs in the context of the sign of Immanuel (vv. 10–25). This passage furthers the interpretation argued in this article. Verses 18–25 contain four ביום ההוא ("on that Day") statements, describing YHWH's purpose to summon Assyria to overtake the land. This invasion serves to realize the judgment portended by Isaiah's son at the beginning of the chapter. While the first two statements are generally recognized as oracles of judgment, the latter two present some interpretive difficulty. Do these verses continue the description of judgment?[47] Or do they shift to a positive note of prosperity?[48]

The crux of the debate falls on the interpretation of verses 21–22. A question raised is whether the mention of curds and honey is an inner-biblical allusion to the glorious land promised to the exodus generation (Exod 3:8; 13:5; Num 13:27). Or does it betray an expectation of a deserted land that reflects the national poverty of Judah? In the larger context of judgment, the latter seems to be more plausible.[49] When all four oracles are taken together, the picture delineates a land that is so desolate from war that the livestock have endless plains to graze with no local populations to interfere. What was once thriving farmland is now only fit for grazing.[50] Though the imagery of curds and honey can itself

---

the section as a whole is conceptually dependent on the connection between the two units (1–9, 10ff.). See Stuart A. Irvine, *Isaiah, Ahaz, and the Syro-Ephraimitic Crisis* (SBLDS 123; Atlanta: Scholars Press, 1990), 159. Irvine rejects the notion that verses 10–17 circulated as an independent oracle, contra Josef Schreiner, *Segen für die Völker. Gesammelte Schriften zur Entstehung und Theologie des Alten Testaments*, ed. Erich Zenger (Würzburg: Echter, 1987), 65–71. Wildberger (Wildberger, *Isaiah 1–12*, 320–21), who views v. 17 as a climactic conclusion to vv. 1–17, segments vv. 18–25 from the rest of the chapter as a weakened expansion of v. 17.

47. So Alison Lo, "Remnant Motif in Amos, Micah, and Zephaniah," in *A God of Faithfulness: Essays in Honour of J. Gordon McConville on His 60th Birthday* (ed. Jamie A. Grant, Alison Lo, and Gordon J. Wenham; New York: T&T Clark, 2011), 130–48. Oswalt (*The Book of Isaiah*, 1:218) primarily understands the reference as negative but does not see the need to deny a positive element.

48. Childs, *Isaiah*, 68; Christopher R. Seitz, *Isaiah 1–39* (Interpretation; Louisville: John Knox, 1993), 80; and William McKane, "The Interpretation of Isaiah VII 14–25," *VT* 17 (1967), 216. Blenkinsopp views the ambiguity of the unit as the result of a later redactional setting reflecting on the Syro-Ephramite threat. See Joseph Blenkinsopp, *A History of Prophecy in Israel* (rev. ed.; Louisville: Westminster John Knox, 1996), 102.

49. Smith, *Isaiah 1–39*, 218; Blenkinsopp, *Isaiah 1–39*, 236; Watts, *Isaiah 1–33*, 145.

50. Edward J. Young, *The Book of Isaiah: The English Text, with Introduction, Exposition, and Notes*, 2nd ed., vol. 1 (NICOT; Grand Rapids: Eerdmans, 1972), 298.

function both in positive and negative contexts, much like the remnant motif, here it is presented negatively.⁵¹ All four ביום ההוא statements thus come together to magnify the coming judgment, furthering the message proclaimed in verses 1–9. Isaiah prophesies a desolate land to demonstrate the Ahaz's folly in distrusting YHWH.

An objection may be raised at this point against a negative interpretation of the chapter that Isaiah's mission is to prophesy the failure of the Syro-Ephramite league, thus offering protection and security for Ahaz. According to this reading, the remnant would accompany the message of hope as the prophet strengthens and encourages the king. Yet, in addition to the points above, the mention of the remnant in this specific context could hardly afford any meaningful comfort. For, the means of disbanding the Syro-Ephramite league is the Assyrian army foretold in the second unit (v. 17ff). Although the nation would provide relief from the imminent threat, they would bring unimaginable destruction upon the land beyond any threat posed by the coalition. Israel, to borrow a metaphor, would escape a lion only to encounter a bear. And as Sheldon Blank states, "Only a remnant can find reassurance in the thought that it is such a remnant."⁵² The contextual data thus lends weight to the remnant used in a negative context as an indication of judgment.⁵³ The faithless response of Ahaz further supports this negative interpretation, standing as the antithesis of the positive characterization of Hezekiah.

Isaiah 37:4, 31–32

Nearly 30 years after the collapse of the Syro-Ephramite coalition, Judah faced the threat of annihilation yet again, but now at the hands of its former deliverer, Assyria. Known for their military ferocity and efficiency, the nation of Assyria claimed a sweeping victory over much of the Near East, reaching into the land of Judah (Isa 36:1). Unlike previous campaigns, Assyria came not to gather tribute of subjugated

---

51. For a survey of the this imagery with similar conclusions, see Etan Levine, "The Land of Milk and Honey," *JSOT* 87 (2000): 43–57. Also, See Nogah Hareuveni, *Nature in Our Biblical Heritage* (trans. Helen Frenkley; Kiryat Ono, Israel: Neot Kedumim, 1980), 11–22. I am thankful to Sam Emadi for directing my attention to this latter reference.

52. Sheldon H. Blank, "The Current Misinterpretation of Isaiah's *She'ar Yashub*," *JBL* 67 (1948), 215. Contra Irvine, *Isaiah, Ahaz, and the Syro-Ephraimitic Crisis*, 146.

53. So Hasel, *The Remnant*, 289.

nations, but to exert total conquest.⁵⁴ With the ascendency of a new king of Assyria, Hezekiah saw an opportunity to sever ties with the nation (cf. 36:4–5). Yet such insubordination would not likely go unpunished. Thus, Sennacherib's army marched against Jerusalem, an event recorded in Isa 36–37.⁵⁵

Sennacherib, through the mediation of his official, the Rabshakeh, called for the surrender of the city in the hearing of the people (36:2–20). Composed of both threat and promise, the Rabshakeh launches a compelling ploy of psychological warfare to make surrender appear the most preferable option.⁵⁶ Reminding the city of Assyria's military success, coupled with the futility of relying on their allies, the Rabshakeh warns against trusting Hezekiah. For, the removal of cultic sites could hardly gain the favor of their national deity. What the Rabshakeh offers, in essence, is a new Solomonic reign of safety and prosperity under the lordship of the king of Assyria (cf. 1 Kgs 4:25). On a natural level, capitulation to Sennacherib was indeed logical, yet Hezekiah's devotion to YHWH precluded such a response.

The first occurrence of the remnant motif in this passage is found in Hezekiah's appeal to Isaiah the prophet for intercession (37:2–4). In the final clause of his request, Hezekiah says, "lift up your prayer for the remnant [השארית] that is left" (37:4f–g).⁵⁷ The function of the remnant motif here, though clearly referencing the current population in Jeru-

---

54. John Bright, *History of Israel* (Louisville: Westminster John Knox, 2000), 271.

55. The relationship between this narrative section and the parallel account in 2 Kgs 18:13–19:37 remains a contentious issue. Yet, a shift has taken place in scholarship away from a view of Isaiah's borrowing source material from 2 Kings, to the priority of the Isaianic text. See K. A. D. Smelik, "Distortion of Old Testament Prophecy: The Purpose of Isaiah Xxxvi and Xxxvii," in *Crises and Perspectives: Studies in Ancient Near Eastern Polytheism, Biblical Theology, Palestinian Archaeology and Intertestamental Literature* (OtSt 24; Leiden: Brill, 1986), 70–106; Christopher R. Seitz, *Zion's Final Destiny: The Development of the Book of Isaiah: A Reassessment of Isaiah 36–39* (Minneapolis: Fortress, 1991), 47–61. Contra Ronald E. Clements, *Old Testament Prophecy: From Oracles to Canon* (Louisville: Westminster John Knox, 1996), 39.

56. Cf. Aarnoud van der Deijl, *Protest or Propaganda: War in the Old Testament Book of Kings and in Contemporaneous Ancient Near Eastern Texts* (SSN 51; Leiden: Brill, 2008), 243.

57. Following 1QIsaᵃ, Watts adopts the reading, "those found in this city" for the conclusion of the verse. See John D. W. Watts, *Isaiah 34–66* (WBC; Dallas: Word, 1987), 32. Surprisingly, Hasel omits discussion of this text in his study.

salem,[58] is not immediately discernible. This plea could either express a positive expectation of hope (i.e., "YHWH has left a remnant to this point, he will certainly deliver us now"), or a desperate cry of despair (i.e., "The destruction Assyria has dealt is so severe that *only* a remnant is left in the land")? Those who immediately label this passage as a positive feature of the plea do not fully appreciate the complexity of the motif itself as shown in this study.[59] As this mention of the remnant awaits a further resolution, it is best to delay interpretation until this complexity is examined.[60]

The clarifying text does indeed occur in the prophet's extended response to Hezekiah's second appeal (37:21–35). The text asserts YHWH's sovereignty over Sennacherib's military conquests. For before Sennacherib had planned his offensive strategy, YHWH had already determined the path of his victory (v. 26). As the one who establishes success in battle, YHWH states his purpose to turn away the threat against Jerusalem and lead Sennacherib away with a hook in his nose and a bit in his mouth (v. 29). Following his address regarding the king of Assyria, YHWH provides a sign for Hezekiah in verse 30, though lacking the miraculous luster one may expect. For two years the city would live off the produce of the land, followed by a year of the normal agricultural cycle. Though this sign may appear quite ordinary, it is upon this guarantee that YHWH pledges a "surviving remnant of the house of Judah [פליטת בית יהודה הנשארה] shall again take root downward and bear fruit upward" (v. 31).

Here in the context of YHWH's promise to prosper the city, the pairing of פליטת and שאר forms a more developed picture of the remnant motif as an indication of blessing. It is interesting to note that in verse 31 the remnant itself is bearing fruit and not simply eating the fruit that had previously grown (v. 30f). Thus Hezekiah is told that YHWH, who will sustain the inhabitants of Jerusalem with the produce of the land, will further plant the remnant as a tree that bears fruit in due time. The combined imagery of roots established in the earth together with the bountiful produce of the vine show the remnant as secure and healthy.

---

58. Oswalt (*The Book of Isaiah*, 1:647) inserts the word "here" at the conclusion of the passage to clarify this point.

59. Willem A. M. Beuken, *Isaiah II* (trans. Brian Doyle; HCOT; Leuven: Peeters, 2000), 358; Smith, *Isaiah 1–39*, 611. Delitzsch (*Isaiah*, 2:93) proposes an unusual interpretation of the motif as establishing a comparison between the sturdy faith of the prophet and the weak faith of the king. Yet, as will be argued, the positive portrayal of Hezekiah stands against this conclusion.

60. So Seitz, *Isaiah 1–39*, 249.

Unlike the vineyard that yielded wild grapes in chapter five, the remnant shall once again be fruitful.

Isaiah makes a further comment securing the blessing pronounced by YHWH in verse 32, once again utilizing a relevant word pair. The verse, opening with a כי conjunction, reasserts the reality of YHWH's promise: a remnant will emerge from Jerusalem. Isaiah declares, "For out of Jerusalem shall go a remnant [שארית], and survivors [פליטה] from Mount Zion" (v. 31a–b).[61] The chiastic construction brackets the remnant lexemes with references to the Holy city. The livelihood of the city is thus linked to the livelihood of the people.[62] In this context, Isaiah uses the remnant motif as an illustration of YHWH's protection and beneficence in response to Hezekiah's faith, which stands in contrast with the negative characterization of Ahaz.[63]

As seen in the narrative texts, Isaiah employs the remnant motif as a literary indicator of the monarchial climate in Judah. When used alongside of a faithless king such as Ahaz, the motif can indicate the severity of judgment that will be brought upon the people. Yet, standing in juxtaposition, the remnant can also display YHWH's purpose to preserve and prosper his people as witness with the faithful Hezekiah. The same literary duality that is evident in the prophetic oracles of the book is also present in the prophetic narrative units.

The Remnant in New Testament Theology

For Christian readers of Scripture, the above understanding of the remnant motif is integral to the interpretation of various New Testament passages (e.g., Matt 24:40–41; Rom 11:5; Rev 11:13). Some of

---

61. Though Hasel views this verse as introducing an eschatological remnant emerging from the historical remnant of the previous verse, such an interpretation does not seem likely for two reasons. First, the conjunction need not be understood as indicating a result as Hasel implicitly argues. More likely, the כי functions assertively, further supporting the promise of YHWH following the sign. Second, Hasel's interpretation fails to view verse 32 in light of YHWH's response to Hezekiah, who asked not for the guarantee of an eschatological remnant, but deliverance of the *current* population. Hence, both verses conjoin to give hope for the inhabitants of Jerusalem at the time of Hezekiah's request as a secure remnant community is announced.

62. As Oswalt (*The Book of Isaiah*, 1:666) states, "if the remnant in Judah is once more to fill the land, then only one outcome is possible—Assyria will not be permitted to enter the city."

63. Lundberg ("Refugees, Survivors and a Community," 34) argues for a neutral interpretation of the remnant motif in chapter 37, yet his analysis misses the contrast between Ahaz and Hezekiah.

these texts clearly bear the marks of a positive literary function of the remnant, while others would seem to retain the negative sense. It is beyond the scope of this article, however, to pursue a thorough analysis of this motif in the New Testament. Thus, Paul's use of Isaiah in Rom 9 will illustrate this point. In Rom 9:27 and 29 Paul cites two texts from Isaiah to support his argument for the continuing faithfulness of God in relation to national Israel. God's promise, says Paul, has not failed, although only a small number of Jews believe. At this point, Paul references Isa 10:22–23 (v. 27) and 1:9 (v. 29) to show that the scant population of ethnic Israelites is not an unprecedented phenomenon. The degree to which Paul intends hope for future national Israel does not concern us here, but rather the hermeneutical presupposition of the interpreter when approaching Paul's use of these texts.[64]

In an article on this passage, John Paul Heil "proposes a much more positive reading of Romans 9:27–29 than is usual."[65] The remnant motif in both the MT and LXX, he claims, is used "as an expression not of a destruction diminishing Israel to 'only' a remnant, but of hope for the future represented by a remnant that will surely issue from Israel."[66] While his conclusion about hope for future Israel, in and of itself, is not my contention, it stems here from a misunderstanding of the two-fold dimension of the remnant motif in the Hebrew text of Isaiah.[67] For how can the promise to Abraham coexist with a message of judgment? As argued above, the remnant in this passage may stand as a warning against faithless nationalism.

---

64. The LXX of Isa 10:22, which reads καὶ ἐὰν γένηται ὁ λαὸς Ισραηλ ὡς ἡ ἄμμος τῆς θαλάσσης, τὸ κατάλειμμα αὐτῶν σωθήσεται, attests to an early interpretation of the motif. Whereas the MT emphasizes the negative sense, the LXX pronounces the salvation of the remnant. Paul's use of Isaiah in Romans in based on the LXX. What concerns us here is not Paul's appropriation of the LXX text as much as the presupposition of the interpreter in reference to the MT. As will be seen, some interpreters conflate the meaning of the LXX and MT when discussing the remnant. While the ultimate interpretation of Romans 9 may vary little on this basis, this article calls for a more nuanced discussion of the Hebrew text.

65. John Paul Heil, "From Remnant to Seed of Hope for Israel: Romans 9:27–29," *CBQ* 64, no. 4 (2002): 703.

66. Ibid., 710. He also maintains that the destruction announced in Isa 10:22 is directed toward Assyria, not Israel.

67. A similar critique is made by David Ian Starling, *Not My People: Gentiles as Exiles in Pauline Hermeneutics* (BZNW 184; Berlin: De Gruyter, 2011), 117 n. 36.

A more nuanced analysis of Paul's use of Isaiah is by Mark Seifrid.[68] He concludes that Paul uses Isaiah typologically to describe the restoration of the remnant. While acknowledging the negative overtones of the Isaianic text,[69] he nevertheless conflates the two senses of the motif in Isa 10:20–21 and 22. For example, regarding verse 22 he states, "In its context in the Hebrew Scriptures the statement undoubtedly promises the salvation of the remnant in the 'righteous overflow' of destruction."[70] Regarding the use of Isa 1:9 in Rom 9:29, Seifrid states, "This rendering takes up the Isaianic theology of the remnant, which portends the restoration of the entire nation."[71] Yet a proper understanding of the remnant theology of Isaiah must take into account both the positive and negative senses.

When assessed in context, the negative sense of the Isaianic passages employed in Rom 9 cannot be dismissed, though, as has been frequently stated in this article, that does not wholly exclude positive implications.[72] As this study has argued, these texts originally served as indications of judgment on the people of Judah. If the present analysis is correct, both Heil and Seifrid's methodological procedures exclude a central component of Isaiah's proclamation.[73]

---

68. Mark Seifrid, "Romans," in *Commentary on the New Testament Use of the Old Testament* (ed. Greg K. Beale and D. A. Carson; Grand Rapids: Baker, 2007), 649.

69. He states, "In the Hoseanic context the language refers to the restoration of Israel after judgment; in the Isaianic setting it describes the nation, which, despite its numbers, will come under divine judgment" (ibid.).

70. Ibid.

71. Ibid., 650. Fitzmyer makes a similar statement: "The preservation of even a remnant is a manifestation of grace." See Joseph A. Fitzmyer, *Romans: A New Translation with Introduction and Commentary* (AB 33; New York: Doubleday, 1993), 575.

72. Moo rightly balances these aspects stating, "Characteristic especially of the prophets, the remnant doctrine contains both a word of judgment and a word of hope." He later concludes, "For Paul also, then, the remnant doctrine confirms his word of judgment to Israel: it is 'not all who are of Israel who are truly Israel.'" See Douglas Moo, *The Epistle to the Romans* (NICNT; Grand Rapids: Eerdmans, 1996), 615.

73. J. Ross Wagner also follows similar methodology to Heil, stating, "The 'remnant' spoken of by Isaiah does not refer to barren survivors destined to die off one by one . . ., but to seed that will germinate, sprout, and blossom into a renewed Israel." See J. Ross Wagner, *Heralds of the Good News: Isaiah and Paul in Concert in the Letter to the Romans* (NovTSup; Leiden: Brill, 2003), 116; also see J. Ross Wagner, "Isaiah in Romans and Galatians," in *Isaiah in the New Testament: The New Testament and the Scriptures of Israel*, (ed. Steve Moyise and Maarten J. J. Menken; London: T&T Clark, 2005), 120–21. Seifrid ("Romans," 650) cites Wagner favorably on this text. Though

Conclusion

This article has argued that the book of Isaiah makes use of a two-fold literary function of the remnant motif, both as an indication of the severity of judgment for Judah and the nations as well as a picture of blessing for Judah. On a literary level, these two aspects dovetail to serve Isaiah's message of the reality of judgment for sin, and hope beyond judgment. Though every occurrence has its own particularities, the remnant motif operates along these parallel paths.

While Isaiah presents a robust use of the motif, other books in the Hebrew Bible certainly contribute to a fuller understanding. Since Hasel's monograph, published in 1974, to my knowledge there has not been a comprehensive analysis of the remnant motif. As Hasel's work itself is marked by issues of its time (e.g., diachronic concerns), a fresh literary analysis would be a welcomed addition. Especially since Hasel's analysis concluded with Isaiah, further research could bridge the motif to the rest of other prophetic books.

The hermeneutical significance of the motif has implications for both the interpretation of Isaiah and other OT books, as well as the New Testament. The neglect of either literary aspect of the remnant, whether positive or negative, can have far-reaching implications in the study of the Hebrew Bible and biblical theology. While the two-fold use of the motif in Isaiah seems clear, further research must bear out its use elsewhere.

Thomas Schreiner has a more positive view of the remnant, he acknowledges the possibility of a negative interpretation. See Thomas R. Schreiner, *Romans* (BECNT; Grand Rapids: Baker, 1998), 529.

THE PIOUS PRAYER OF AN IMPERFECT PROPHET: THE PSALM OF JONAH IN ITS NARRATIVE CONTEXT

IAN J. VAILLANCOURT

Wycliffe College, University of Toronto
ian.vaillancourt@mail.utoronto.ca

The question of whether the psalm of Jonah 2 is integrative or disruptive in its narrative context greatly effects one's interpretation of the book of Jonah as a whole. While the older historical-critical scholars have almost universally concluded that the psalm of Jonah was a disruptive addition to an otherwise coherent narrative, more recent canonical interpreters have tended to argue for its integrative nature. Utilizing the canonical method of interpretation, this article freshly evaluates the issues and argues for the integrative nature of the psalm of Jonah in its narrative context by exploring: 1) comparative vocabulary between psalm and narrative in Jonah; 2) the phenomenon of Hebrew poetry inserted into narrative; 3) the psalm's contribution to the theme of irony in Jonah; 4) the psalm of Jonah in the broader context of the Book of the Twelve; and 5) a rethinking of the problem of Jonah's conflicted character between psalm and narrative.

KEYWORDS: *Jonah, Canonical, Characterization, Integrative, Narrative, Psalm*

INTRODUCTION

The psalm of Jonah has been the focus of scholarly attention for two thousand years, and scholarly debate for two hundred years,[1] or as Trible put it, "[e]voking a great storm over the centuries, the eight-verse poem

---

1. Watts notes that, "The relation between the narrative and the psalm in the book of Jonah has been studied and discussed more than any other psalm in a narrative context." James W. Watts, *Psalm and Story: Inset Hymns in Hebrew Narrative* (JSOTSup 139; Sheffield: JSOT Press, 1992), 132.

threatens to swallow the forty-verse narrative."[2] The book of Jonah as a whole seems to see-saw back and forth between "the bad Jonah" and "the good Jonah," with the psalm as the prime example of the prophet's piety. The book opens with a surprising note of role reversal, as "the bad Jonah" disobeys the word of YHWH and is ultimately cast into the deep, while "the good Gentile sailors" cast themselves on YHWH's mercy, fear him with a great fear, recognize his sovereign pleasure, sacrifice to him, and vow vows to him. But in the psalm of Jonah 2 the prophet *seems* to have caught up to the spiritual stature of these Gentiles, as "the good Jonah" is mercifully swallowed by a great fish, prays a model prayer, and promises a sacrifice of thanksgiving and the fulfillment of vows to YHWH. The reported words of the prophet are a well-constructed psalm of thanksgiving, with some praise elements as well.[3] This psalm is filled with words and phrases that are common in the Psalter,[4] and it focuses vividly on Jonah's desperate circumstances; however, it is told from the perspective of one who looks back on deliverance. It seems certain that these pious words are included in the book because "the good Jonah" is an example to follow. With the psalm freshly in mind, the reader's perception of "the good Jonah" of chapter 3 is only amplified, for after his ejection from the fish the prophet obeys YHWH, announces judgment to Nineveh, and witnesses nationwide repentance by magisterial decree. But the story does not end there: in chapter 4 "the bad Jonah" resurfaces, this time as the sulking prophet who never really wanted Israel's enemies to be objects of YHWH's mercy in the first place. If the book begins with a word of command from YHWH to Jonah about his call to preach in Nineveh, it ends with a word of correction from YHWH to Jonah about his sovereign right to pity Nineveh.

Even this cursory overview of the book has raised questions about the psalm. Why a psalm of thanksgiving and not lament: was Jonah not still in distress in the belly of the fish? Are model words of piety appropriate from the lips of a prophet whose heart will later be displayed as still hard and rebellious? What about the language: do expressions that

---

2. Phyllis Trible, *Rhetorical Criticism: Context, Method, and the Book of Jonah* (Minneapolis: Fortress, 1994), 173.

3. Although the psalm contains a great deal of lament, the perspective of the psalmist is one of looking back on deliverance. See Hermann Gunkel and Joachim Begrich, *Introduction to Psalms: The Genres of the Religious Lyric of Israel* (trans. James D. Nogalski; Macon, GA: Mercer University Press, 1998), 201–02, 340–41.

4. As noted in Brevard S. Childs, *Introduction to the Old Testament as Scripture* (Philadelphia: Fortress, 1979), 423; Hans Walter Wolff, *Obadiah and Jonah: A Commentary* (trans. Margaret Kohl; Minneapolis: Augsburg, 1986), 133.

have more parallels in the Psalter than in the Jonah narrative belong in this book? In short, why is the seemingly disruptive psalm in the book at all? Without the psalm "the bad Jonah" of chapter 4 is less of a surprise and could possibly indicate that the prophet's preaching ministry in chapter 3 was the result of coercion by YHWH rather than true heart change. Is there a reasonable solution that explains the placement of the psalm in its broader narrative context?

In what follows I will explore these issues by showing first that pre-critical interpreters had already begun to ask these kinds of questions, even as they assumed the book's coherence. Next, I will summarize the most popular historical-critical answers to the question. This will set the stage for the main focus of the article, in which I employ the canonical approach as a helpful means of explaining the integrative nature of the psalm in a unified book of Jonah. Although some interpreters have focused their energy on arguments for or against the psalm as *original* to the book, and others have reasoned for or against *redactional unity* in Jonah, I will focus my attention on the question of the psalm as *integrative or disruptive*, without commenting on the text's prehistory.[5] In so doing I will glean insights from those who argue along the lines of authorial or redactional unity/disunity while maintaining a focus on the question of whether the interpreter may approach the book of Jonah as a meaningful and coherent, and indeed inspired whole.[6]

THE PSALM OF JONAH AND THE HISTORY OF INTERPRETATION

Although the dominant assumption throughout the history of interpretation has been that the psalm in Jonah 2 is original and essential to the prophetic book as a whole, difficult questions relating to the unity of the

---

5. This appropriation of the canonical approach differs slightly from Childs, for although he viewed the final form of the biblical text as primary in a culminating way, he still often asserted his own theories about the text's prehistory. In the case of the book of Jonah, Childs believed the psalm was a secondary insertion, and that the canonical shaping offered an integrative, though altered message for the book as a whole. He went so far as to posit a lack of evidence for two versions of the story that were separated by a long historical development, implying that the stages of redaction must have been close together. See Childs, *Introduction to the Old Testament as Scripture*, 425. In my appropriation of the canonical approach I desire to spend less time on theories of the text's prehistory because of their speculative nature.

6. This explains why I will interact appreciatively with, for example, Watts, throughout the latter portion of this article, despite the fact that I am not arguing along the lines of redactional unity, but rather, the integrative nature of the book of Jonah with the psalm included, without comment on the text's prehistory.

book had also been considered prior to the rise of enlightenment hermeneutics. In addition to the debated question of how to best interpret the psalm,[7] in the Middle Ages ibn Ezra observed that the fish was female in 2:2 but male in 2:11, and that the language in between reflected present and past deliverance. However, he explained the latter as a sort of "prophetic perfect tense," because the prophetic mind regarded the prayer to have been answered even before the salvation was accomplished.[8] In the Reformation period, Luther struggled with how one could compose a psalm while in the belly of a fish and concluded that Jonah did not pray these very words with his lips, as "his mood when surrounded by this horrible death was not so cheerful as to compose such a fine song."[9] Instead, for Luther this psalm was a later work of praise and thanksgiving by Jonah, which recorded how he felt at the time of being swallowed by the fish.[10] Finally, contrary to a positive view of Jonah's three-day retreat in the depths, Calvin saw the fish as tantamount to hell or the grave, but that even there Jonah gathered courage, an example of faith.[11] For Calvin as with Luther, though Jonah's prayer was not composed in the words now related, these words relate the thoughts in Jonah's mind when he was in the belly of the fish.[12]

At the hinge between pre-critical and critical interpreters, George Adam Smith interacted directly with critical views, noting the parallels with the Psalter, along with the prayer's unique features, before declaring

---

7. For example, Basil ignored its thanksgiving elements and assumed Jonah was crying for help; Gregory of Nazianzus set forth Jonah's endurance in prayer as a model of Christian piety and his fate in the fish's belly was a sign of salvation; Cassiodorus saw Jonah's psalm as a place of repentance, Theodoret, a place that typified Christ's three days in the tomb, Symeon, a place where Jonah cried out and God heard and delivered him. For Tertullian, Jonah's expulsion from the whale after three days typified Christ's resurrection. See *The Twelve Prophets* (ed. Alberto Ferreiro and Thomas C. Oden; ACCS; Downers Grove: InterVarsity, 2003), 136–40; Joseph Blenkinsopp, *A History of Prophecy in Israel* (Louisville: Westminster John Knox, 1996), 240–41.

8. As noted in Athalya Brenner, "Jonah's Poem Out of and Within Its Context," in *Among the Prophets: Language, Image, and Structure in the Prophetic Writings* (ed. Philip R. Davies and David J. A. Clines; Sheffield: JSOT, 1993), 186–87, and R. Reed Lessing, *Jonah* (CC; St. Louis: Concordia, 2007), 174.

9. Martin Luther, *Lectures on the Minor Prophets II: Jonah Habakkuk* (ed. Hilton C. Oswald; trans. C. Froelich; Luther's Works; Saint Louis: Concordia, 1974), 70.

10. Ibid., 71.

11. See John Calvin, *Commentaries on the Twelve Minor Prophets, Volume III: Jonah, Micah, Nahum* (trans. John Owen; Grand Rapids, MI: Eerdmans, 1950), 74.

12. See Ibid., 75.

that it was original to the author[13] (whether originally composed by him or not), and inserted from his perspective of the fish as the point of Jonah being saved. Smith also agreed with Luther that a man in Jonah's position could not have composed or even compiled such a psalm. He further asserted that the spirit of the psalm was national, in conformity with the truth underlying the book.[14]

THE PSALM OF JONAH IN HISTORICAL-CRITICAL SCHOLARSHIP

Phyllis Trible notes that while there are no major text-critical problems in the book of Jonah, historical-critical interpreters have struggled without resolution to determine the book's author, date, setting, and purpose, with the psalm in Jonah 2 as a major source of tension.[15] Over the past two hundred years, the dominant conclusion from historical-critical scholarship has been that the psalm of Jonah was a disruptive later interpolation, and that it serves no ultimate purpose in the flow or plot of the book.[16] The eight most common arguments from this school of thought are as follows:

1) A psalm of lament rather than thanksgiving would better fit the context of chapter 1.

2) The psychological picture of Jonah in chapters 1, 2, and 4 is markedly different from the pious Jonah of chapter 2.

---

13. Although my focus in this article is not on the text's prehistory, when I am reporting the view of another interpreter I will sometimes comment on their view along these lines; hence the use of the term "original" in this instance.

14. See George Adam Smith, *The Book of the Twelve Prophets, Commonly Called the Minor, Volume II: Zephaniah, Nahum, Habakkuk, Obadiah, Haggai, Zechariah, Malachi, Joel, Jonah* (London: Hodder and Stoughton, 1906), 499–501.

15. See Trible, *Rhetorical Criticism*, 107–08.

16. According to Holbert, one of the first critical commentators to argue that the Psalm of Jonah was a part of the original composition (though not original to the book), was Landes. See J. C. Holbert, "'Deliverance Belongs to Yahweh!': Satire in the Book of Jonah," *JSOT* 21 (1981): 70.

3) It is odd to find the Jonah who had to be coerced into any speech by pagans in chapter 1, to be voluntarily in prayer in chapter 2.[17]

4) The psalm was out of step with Jonah's prophetic task.

5) The psalm should appear after Jonah's deliverance from the fish and not before.

6) The vocabulary of psalm and narrative are markedly different in Jonah.

7) The drowning language must be metaphorical as it is in other psalms.

8) The psalm interrupts the overarching pattern of the book.[18]

In short, proponents of this view believe the psalm to be a *disruptive* later addition that does not fit into the narrative of Jonah.

Hans Walter Wolff is a thoughtful representative of those who take this critical position with regard to the psalm. I choose to interact with him because he is often extremely insightful, as displayed in his discussion of the dating of the book, his setting of Jonah in the context of the Twelve, and his discussion of the intentional caricature of Jonah by the book's author.[19]

In the end, though, Wolff cites six reasons why the psalm of Jonah was not incorporated into the text by the original author, with the implication that it is disruptive, rather than integrative, in the context of the book as a whole:[20]

1) The psalm is said fit a setting of the temple much better than a fish's belly.

---

17. These first three common arguments in favor of the disruptive nature of the psalm were taken from Landes (who will later argue for the originality of the psalm) and summarized in Holbert, "'Deliverance Belongs to Yahweh!'" 70.

18. The last five common arguments in favor of the disruptive nature of the psalm were taken from Watts, *Psalm and Story*, 141. Note that Watts is not a proponent of this view, but his summary of the position is helpful.

19. See Wolff, *Obadiah and Jonah*, 75–178.

20. See Ibid., 78–79; 128–31.

2) With regard to language, the prayers in the narrative are said to address God alone (O YHWH), but never talk about him. Further to this, Wolff notes that different words are used to describe the petitioner's distress in psalm and narrative in Jonah, and that גדול ("great") is used 14 times in the narrative but not at all in the psalm.

3) The characterization of Jonah is problematic for Wolff, as the psalm of Jonah "presents the reader with a Jonah who has repented in the most exemplary way"—a Jonah who for Wolff is not found at the end of the ancient prose narrative.

4) The agent of Jonah's trip into the sea is reported differently: the narrative identifies the seamen and in the psalm it is YHWH.

5) The timing of the song of thanksgiving: in reality one needs to be in the sanctuary, but Jonah is far from the sanctuary.

6) The intended audience who will be instructed by the psalm: the construct chain הבלי־שוא ("meaningless emptiness")[21] would suggest that it is directed to correct those who do not worship YHWH, but the fact that these "idol worshippers" forsake their חסד ("steadfast love") shows that they were formerly Yahwists.

Wolff continues:

> Even when, in the following passage, the narrator can talk about an obedient Jonah for a time, his "hero" remains as coldly reserved and taciturn as he was in chap. 1. But at the end his initial reluctance actually builds up to a sulky defiance that makes him want to die rather than submit. No, the man in the psalm, who prostrates himself before God in thanksgiving, and rejoices at being able to tell his brothers what he has experienced, is quite a different person—a later person.[22]

Wolff concludes that the book of Jonah is best interpreted with the psalm extracted. On this model the fish swallows Jonah, Jonah stays there for three days and nights, he preaches in Nineveh after his ejection from the

---

21. See the discussion of this term in what follows.

22. Ibid., 130.

fish, and his heart is revealed to have never been changed as he sulks in chapter 4.[23]

Inexplicably though, for Wolff the psalm does have meaning. The addition of the psalm is said to show that the mercy of God can turn the belly of hell into the womb of a new birth.[24] Without explanation, then, the disruptive interpolation is somehow relevant devotionally. However, in the end Wolff will still conclude that present day exegesis of Jonah need not be burdened with any explanation of the psalm—for him, the interpreter ought to focus on the narrative flow with the psalm extracted and ignored.[25] But is this the best explanation?

THE PSALM OF JONAH AS INTEGRATIVE IN THE BOOK OF JONAH

While the historical-critical method of interpretation employed by Wolff is most concerned with reconstructing the text's pre-history, canonical interpreters are most concerned with the message of the final form of the text. Like historical-critics, canonical interpreters *consider* the text's pre-history, but with caution as a speculative and theoretical enterprise.[26] They make a theological decision in favor of the final form presentation as the proper parameter for interpretation, rather than the simple history of the text's development as it is reconstructed by historical critics.[27] In our specific case, the canonical approach *gives the psalm a chance* to

---

23. See Ibid., 131. Though on different grounds, Trible (*Rhetorical Criticism*, 172) agrees, claiming that rhetorical-critical analysis, "supports source critical findings that deem the psalm a secondary addition to the narrative." She goes on to argue on the basis of the narrative as a complete literary unit, and the disruptive nature of the psalm (in terms of the symmetry of the book). See ibid., 172–73.

24. See Wolff, *Obadiah and Jonah*, 88, citing Uwe Steffen, *Das Mysterium Von Tod und Auferstehung. Formen und Wandlungen Des Jona-Motivs, Etc.* (Göttingen: Vandenhoeck & Ruprecht, 1963), 106. Also a legitimate application for Wolff, Jonah's time in the belly of the fish became a type, or prefiguration of the fate of Jesus, and the church herself can learn from this scene. In addition, Wolff adds, "Very many groups within the church deserve no more than to be devoured and spat out; and yet the church must not forget the playful triumph of her God who, in spite of it all, still makes her serviceable and ready to set out at long last on the way to Nineveh" (*Obadiah and Jonah*, 142).

25. George M. Landes notes this in "The Kerygma of the Book of Jonah: The Contextual Interpretation of the Jonah Psalm," *Int* 21 (1967): 6.

26. See Christopher R. Seitz, "Canonical Approach," in *Dictionary for Theological Interpretation of the Bible* (ed. Kevin J. Vanhoozer, et. al.; Grand Rapids: Baker Academic, 2005), 100.

27. See Ibid., 101.

show itself as integrative in the flow of the book of Jonah, and this "innocent until proven guilty" attitude will prove fruitful as we progress.[28] In what follows I will look at the issue of vocabulary, the phenomenon of psalms inserted into Hebrew narrative, the theme of irony in Jonah, the book of Jonah in the context of the Twelve, and a rethinking of the so-called problem of the inconsistent character of Jonah. In so doing, I will omit the question of whether the psalm was original to the author of the book of Jonah and will replace this question about the text's prehistory with a consideration of the psalm's integrative or disruptive nature in the flow of the book as a whole.

Vocabulary

Although the psalm and the narrative in Jonah do exhibit differing vocabulary, Watts notes that there are also some similarities, with קרא ("to call");[29] the mention of sacrifices and vows,[30] and the verb ירד ("to go down") as compared to Jonah's downward motion throughout the early narrative,[31] among other examples.[32] Even where the vocabulary differs, one must not forget that in its very nature Hebrew poetry uses more diverse language than Hebrew prose.[33] One should *not expect*, therefore, the vocabulary or the ethos of psalm and narrative to match. In addition, it needs to be remembered that the psalm of Jonah does not need to be an original composition of the author of Jonah in order to be integrative in the context of the book. For example, a plausible solution

---

28. After rehearsing the major source-critical arguments in favor of the psalm as neither composed nor included by the author of the narrative, Trible notes that the debate has subsequently "swum around" to the "dry land" of traditional formulation, with the subjectivity of the debate finally resulting in views that now "turn on their circuit" back-and-forth between the two positions. See Trible, *Rhetorical Criticism*, 160–61.

29. See 2:3; cf. 1:2, 6, 14; 3:2.

30. Cf. the זבח ("sacrifice") and נדר ("vow") Jonah promises as reflected in the sailor's reaction to the calming of the sea; 2:10; cf. 1:16.

31. See 2:7; 1:3, 5.

32. Watts further notes that the prose introduction to the psalm (2:2) echoes the introduction of Jonah's prayer in 4:2, with the two prayers also sharing vocabulary חסד ("steadfast love") in 2:9 and 4:2; חיי ("my life") and נפשי ("my soul") in 2:7–8 and 4:2–3. But also of note are the *different* words used between psalm and narrative to describe "the sea," and being "inside" (the ship, the belly of Sheol). See Watts, *Psalm and Story*, 133–35.

33. See Douglas Stuart, *Hosea–Jonah*, (WBC 31; Grand Rapids: Zondervan, 1988), 439.

could be that in his reported speech, the prophet was viewed as citing a preexisting psalm in the belly of the fish, much the same as worshipers through the centuries have used the biblical psalms to express their own praise, thanks, and laments.[34] The idea that this could have been a preexisting psalm written originally for another (cultic?) context does not preclude it from being meaningfully incorporated into the text of Jonah.

The Art of Hebrew Poetry Inserted into Narrative

Lacking in much of the discussion about the psalm of Jonah in the narrative flow of the book is a broader analysis of this phenomenon throughout the Hebrew Bible. With the 1992 publication of *Psalm and Story: Inset Hymns in Hebrew Narrative*, James W. Watts has provided interpreters with a valuable resource in this regard. He notes that the mixing of prose and poetry is a distinctive literary feature of the Hebrew Bible, where books that are primarily prose interrupt the narrative sequence with the insertion of poems.[35] Many (but certainly not all) of these poems are very similar to the contents of the Psalter and share some common features among themselves, most notably they often occupy thematically climactic and structurally crucial positions in larger blocks of narrative.[36] These psalms are spoken by the characters in the narrative rather than the narrator, and although the internal evidence of the psalms suggests that they once existed in the cult, they are presented in non-cultic contexts in their new narrative context.[37] Throughout his analysis Watts shows that a given inset psalm could be deleted without being missed in the narrative flow, but this points to the fact that *it was not meant to be used for plot development* but for other narrative purposes such as thematic exposition and characterization, a practice consistent with the other ancient Near Eastern cultures. Therefore, a psalm's failure to develop the plot does not necessarily indicate that it is disruptive in the

---

34. This point is also made in Landes, "The Kerygma of the Book of Jonah," 8–9.

35. See Watts, *Psalm and Story*, 11.

36. Note that Watts believes most of these inset psalms show signs of being later additions to the narratives in which they are now found. In his view, evidence of this includes, "textual disturbances around the psalms, thematic conflicts between the psalms and the prose narratives, and in one case, an edition of the narrative in which the psalm is missing." See ibid., 11–12.

37. See ibid., 12.

context of its biblical book!³⁸ For Watts, whereas prose narrative eschews direct commentary, poetry offers vivid descriptions of feelings and emphatic statements of ideas. Therefore,

> [when] writers or editors of narrative needed to make thematic emphases and emotions explicit, they did not try to reproduce the effects of poetry in prose, but simply switched modes. Explicit emotional displays and interior characterization were thus introduced into Hebrew narrative without changing its basic nature.³⁹

For Watts it was natural, then, for the authors of Hebrew narrative to turn to psalmody in order to deepen the characterization of the figures in the narrative.⁴⁰

Watts then deals specifically with the psalm of Jonah. He notes that the prior and subsequent narrative plot contains no direct references to the psalm, with the possible exception of 2:11—if YHWH's order to the fish was *a response* to the psalm, which is only possible if the fish is viewed as an agent of rescue from drowning rather than a further deterioration in Jonah's condition.⁴¹ Further, it has already been shown that there are verbal and thematic links between the psalm and the narrative.⁴² Although many wrestle with the "two Jonahs" between psalm and narrative, Watts shows that the picture of YHWH is consistent between them, and therefore the characterization of Jonah deserves to be taken seriously as well.⁴³ He adds that Jonah's piety in the psalm accords with that expressed by him in his narrative speeches, from his orthodox confession to the sailors (1:9) to his accurate diagnosis of the cause of the storm (1:12), and the reason he gives for his disobedience to YHWH (4:2). It is therefore clear to Watts that, "the psalm accords with the

---

38. See ibid., 34, 83 (song of Deborah), 100, 108 (song of David). Stuart adds that in any narrative, large chunks can be removed without doing damage to what remains: e.g., deleting 10–20 percent of the Gospels, Psalms, Deuteronomy, or Isaiah. See Stuart, *Hosea–Jonah*, 438.

39. Watts, *Psalm and Story*, 194.

40. See ibid., 131.

41. See ibid., 133.

42. See section on vocabulary above; ibid., 132–35.

43. See ibid., 136–38.

narrative in characterizing Jonah as an orthodox Yahwist."[44] Although there is tension, then, between the narrative and the psalm in Jonah, the narrative role of the psalm is said to focus on characterization.[45] As for the supposed need for a lament where a psalm of thanksgiving is found, Watts adds that, "individual thanksgivings tend to be placed at a point in the narrative when deliverance is expected, but not yet accomplished."[46] Therefore, the psalm's position or genre is no reason to conclude that it must be disruptive in the book as a whole.[47] The psalm of Jonah, like Exod 15, is used to evoke reader identification with the characters in the narrative; and like 2 Sam 22 and Isa 38, to provide inner characterization.[48] In fact, although these things could have been accomplished without a psalm in a modern novel, "in Hebrew literature deep inner characterization and the close reader identification that it can engender are usually reserved for poetry."[49] Far from being a clumsy interpolation that lacks sense, a book of Jonah that includes the psalm is powerfully applied to the reader. And far from being merely a device for aesthetic pleasure or midrashic interpretation, the psalm does contribute to the narrative through its position in the book and its thematic contents.[50] Since plot development is not the primary criteria for evaluating a psalm's narrative role, and since the narrative's themes can be altered and enhanced with such poems, one should not be hasty to dismiss their interpretive value.[51]

Irony

Many have noted the theme of irony in the book of Jonah. For example, Hauser has shown that Jonah's name, which means "dove," adds an element of surprise to the book, as the themes through chapters 1–3 of

---

44. Ibid., 138.

45. See ibid., 140.

46. Ibid., 141–42. cf. Hezekiah's Psalm, Daniel's Praise, and the Song of the Three.

47. See ibid., 141–42.

48. See ibid., 143.

49. Ibid., 144.

50. See ibid., 186.

51. See ibid., 190.

flight, submission to the sacrificial cult, and beauty all seem to fit various nuances of the dove image, but this "fit" grinds to a sudden halt in chapter 4.[52] However, is there a purpose in this contrast? Is the irony purposeful and intentional?

We have already noticed verbal links between psalm and narrative in Jonah, but a phrase from Jonah 2:9 adds to the theme of irony and helps display its purpose. In Jonah 2:9 we read that "those who regard הבלי־שוא ['meaningless emptiness,' or something similar] forsake their חסד ['steadfast love']." Many have noted that the terms are used together in Ps 31:7 and that הבלי ("meaningless") is in parallel with "idols" in Deut 32:21.[53] But is it possible that the terms have connotations of idolatry, and are also purposefully broad to include the earlier actions of Jonah (from ch. 1) which he now regrets, as well as those he would return to later in the book (in ch. 4), thus forming an intentional ironic contrast between the repentant Jonah of 2:9 and the clearly disobedient Jonah of chapter 4? Especially as these words are coupled with the covenantal term חסד ("steadfast love"), there seems to be room for such an interpretation. A broad look at the use of the terms throughout the Hebrew Bible shows clearly that they can both refer to idols or what idols do, but they are also broad terms. In the context of Jonah, perhaps it is better to favor Simon's general translation of "empty folly."[54] This would only add to the parabolic/ironic function of Jonah. If the Jonah of the psalm resolves to never succumb to empty folly, the Jonah of chapter 4 has done just that, for in his own self-deception his false views of the proper object of YHWH's grace and mercy have surfaced. The reader of the book of Jonah has journeyed with Jonah, and so has been led to identify with "the pious Jonah's" prayer in 2:9, only to be rebuked along with "the impious Jonah" in chapter 4. In this way the prayer of Jonah 2 functions in a similar way as Nathan's ewe lamb story in 2 Sam 12, and the words of YHWH to Jonah in chapter 4 correspond to Nathan's "you are the man." In other words, the reader is first drawn in to relate to Jonah as a pious worshiper in Jonah 2 who would never forsake their חסד ("steadfast love") by following empty folly before being rebuked along with Jonah in chapter 4 for doing just that in a way they had not seen in themselves previously. Without the psalm of Jonah,

---

52. See Alan Jon Hauser, "Jonah: In Pursuit of the Dove," *JBL* 104 (1985): 22–23.

53. See, for example, Wolff, *Obadiah and Jonah*, 127.

54. See Uriel Simon, *Jonah* (JPS; ed. Michael Fishbane; trans. Lenn Schramm; Philadelphia: Jewish Publication Society, 1999), 23–24. Alternatively, Stuart (*Hosea–Jonah*, 468) translates the terms as "empty nothings."

which highlights Jonah's resolve and his allegiance to YHWH, the fall of Jonah in chapter 4 would lose its force, and the parabolic/ironic function of the book would vanish. The psalm powerfully adds, then, to both the irony and the kerygmatic purpose of the book for the Israelite people.

Clues from the Context of the Book of the Twelve

Although many commentators approach the book of Jonah as an individual work,[55] more recently there has been a canonical movement which appreciates the final form of prophetic books, including the Book of the Twelve as a unit.[56] Seitz notes that this movement is concerned, "to show that the Twelve is a single coordinated work as well as a composite collection,"[57] and therefore, "outfitted to speak both as twelve and as one."[58] Already in the early second century B.C.E., Sirach refers to the twelve prophets as a unit (Sir 49:10), the Qumran manuscripts have them collected into one scroll, and many other early witnesses do the same.

In Book of the Twelve scholarship, the catchword is often seen as binding books together, and Dempster points out that Obadiah succeeds Amos and deals with Edom, Jonah deals with repentance and salvation in Nineveh, Micah predicts judgment on Assyria, and Nahum describes the fall of an unrepentant Nineveh.[59] The Book of the Twelve

---

55. For example, in Collins's standard *Introduction to the Hebrew Bible*, he deals with Jonah outside of his section on the prophets, grouped with Ruth, Esther, Tobit, and Judith in a chapter called, "prose fiction." See John J. Collins, *Introduction to the Hebrew Bible* (Minneapolis: Fortress, 2004), 536. Seitz also notes that whereas Jonah is placed fifth in the canonical presentation (MT) of the Twelve, Blenkinsopp and von Rad (and others) put him last in their analyses. See Christopher R. Seitz, *Prophecy and Hermeneutics: Toward a New Introduction to the Prophets* (Grand Rapids: Baker Academic, 2007), 140. For a helpful overview of the rise of higher criticism and its application to the prophets, see ibid., 75–87.

56. See ibid., 18.

57. Ibid., 30.

58. Christopher R. Seitz, *The Goodly Fellowship of the Prophets: The Achievement of Association in Canon Formation* (Grand Rapids: Baker Academic, 2009), 88. In that same place Seitz goes so far as to suggest that, "it is questionable whether individual books of the Twelve had much of an individual life." For his full explanation, see ibid., 110.

59. See Stephen G. Dempster, *Dominion and Dynasty: A Biblical Theology of the Hebrew Bible* (NSBT; Downers Grove: InterVarsity, 2003), 183. See also Seitz, *Prophecy and Hermeneutics*, 120–21; Seitz adds that Jonah follows Obadiah, and so, "the account of Edom and the nations in Obadiah affects our understanding of God's dealings

as a whole, then, offers a more full-orbed picture of this foreign nation than the individual books could accomplish on their own.

From the perspective of a unified Book of the Twelve, a unified book of Jonah also adds to the multifaceted message.[60] If the Day of YHWH will figure in as a day of great judgment, the book of Jonah is clear that if those nations repent, YHWH will relent from the disaster he plans to send them, a theme applied to Israel in Hosea.[61] On the other hand, if those repentant nations will cease to diligently seek YHWH, then Nahum makes clear that they will undergo judgment.

I have already shown that the psalm of Jonah intensifies the theme of irony in the book, adding to its parabolic/ironic use among the people of Israel. From this perspective, the book of Jonah shows that even the most sincere member of the covenant community can experience inner rebellion against YHWH's mercy to their enemies, and that the member of the covenant community must be as excited about YHWH's mercy (cf. Exod 34:6–7) *to the nations* as they are when it comes to the people of Israel.

Finally, although it is not in line with a direct keyword link, within the Twelve as a collection, Jonah can also be seen as a counterpart to Habakkuk. If Habakkuk needed correction from YHWH (cf. 1:5), then Jonah needed to be rebuked! But both prophets are also set forth as pious

---

with the nations in what lies ahead in the canonical depiction of the Minor Prophets as a whole" (139–40). He notes further that the theme of the repentance of the Ninevites, both human and animal in Jonah (3:8), has its counterpart in Joel 1:20, where even the wild beasts cry to YHWH because the water brooks are dried up. See ibid., 148.

60. Seitz (ibid., 119) agrees: "Jonah is a special case whose interpretation follows best when a sense of the larger conceptuality of the arrangement of the Twelve as a whole is grasped."

61. For more observations along these lines, see especially Marvin A. Sweeny, "Sequence and Interpretation in the Book of the Twelve," in *Reading and Hearing the Book of the Twelve* (ed. James Nogalski and Marvin A. Sweeney; Atlanta: SBL, 2000), 63; Rolf Rendtorff, "How to Read the Book of the Twelve As a Theological Unity," in *Reading and Hearing the Book of the Twelve*, 82–83; Paul R. House, "The Character of God in the Book of the Twelve," in *Reading and Hearing the Book of the Twelve*, 134. Seitz (*Prophecy and Hermeneutics*, 170) adds, "What if, for example, it could be shown that the primary context of interpretation for the book of Jonah is the book of the Twelve, wherein it operates as its own book, but also as a commentary on the dense theological confession that YHWH is compassionate and merciful, but also will by no means clear the guilty.... This theme cuts with special force when one considers Israel's relationship to the nations and God's forbearance and justice vis-à-vis them and vis-à-vis his chosen people Israel, not just in general terms (as in the case of Jonah), but also in terms of the final-form arrangement of the book of the Twelve."

singers of psalms whom the covenant people ought to imitate.[62] The lives of both of these prophets will correct the covenant member in their approach to YHWH (whether mildly in Habakkuk or strongly in Jonah), as well as offer them pious words for their own prayers. What an encouragement within the Twelve that if at least two prophets needed mild or strong correction, the reader may also approach YHWH, gracious and compassionate, in the midst of their own failings.

Rethinking The Problem of Jonah's "Dual Character"

This leads to the question of the so-called dual characterization of Jonah between psalm and narrative, and particularly between chapters 2 and 4 of the book.[63] However, that there is wavering, imperfect faith in Jonah does not preclude the idea that the psalm is integrative in the flow of the book. It would seem very two-dimensional to claim that every person is either "good," and always acting as such, or "bad," and always acting as such, or that the Bible always portrays its main characters as heroes to imitate and never fools to learn from. In fact, we meet other such conflicted characters throughout the Hebrew Bible. For the sake of space, I will briefly explore two of these figures, one from Hebrew narrative that also includes poetic text and one from Hebrew narrative that does not include any poetic text. These brief descriptions will serve to confirm that the Hebrew Bible is replete with figures who are more complicated than simply "good" or "bad" and that the real hero of the Old Testament is YHWH. They will also show that perceived differences in characterization are not only found in prose versus poetry, but also in narratives themselves. Dual, or competing, characterization is not the issue, then, but the use of different modes to communicate different aspects of a figure's character.

David is the obvious choice as an example of a figure whose life is presented in Hebrew narrative that also contains poetic material.[64]

---

62. See Ibid., 146, 243.

63. Contrary to most, Trible (*Rhetorical Criticism*, 171–72) sees the psalm as negative and not positive, with Jonah's words of deliverance received in the psalm as a proclamation of his arrogance. I am not, however, persuaded by her argument, as the five points in this section make clear.

64. Moses (and the poetic text in Exod 15) and Hezekiah (and the praise in Isa 38) are two other figures whose descriptions in narrative also contain inset psalms. Moses and Hezekiah are also two complicated figures who exhibit great victories and great failures, and in both cases their failures appear in material subsequent to their reported pious poetic songs.

Aside from the material in Chronicles or the 73 psalms attributed to him, in the narratives of 1 and 2 Samuel David is linked to *two* psalms that have been inserted into Hebrew narrative.[65] In addition, the narrative portions of Samuel clearly present David as a complicated figure who exhibits flaws and faith from beginning to end.[66] In other words, these texts all combine to present an integrative rather than a disruptive portrait of David between portions of narrative and between narrative and inset psalms.

First, at David's anointing the use of a horn of oil (1 Sam 16:1, 13; cf. 1 Sam 2:10) links him to the song of Hannah and the prophecy that YHWH will give strength to his king and exalt the horn of his anointed one.[67] He is clearly presented, then, as the hoped-for monarch who will be YHWH's instrument of victory for his people, as set forth in the poetic overture to the books of Samuel. Then, near the end of 2 Samuel David is recorded as singing a song of thanksgiving to YHWH (1 Sam 22), which could have closed the account of his life on a high note. However, *after* the recorded words of this psalm, the narrative will present David as taking a census of the people and those same people will bear the consequences of his sin in the form of a mass execution by YHWH, before the book finally closes with an account of David's repentance. The narrative of his life will indeed present David as the great king of Israel, as the anointed of YHWH (1 Sam 16) who defeats the enemy of God's people on their behalf (1 Sam 17), and as the righteous suffering one who refuses to put YHWH's anointed to death despite suffering greatly at his hand (1 Sam 18–31). He will be the recipient of the great promises of 2 Sam 7 (referred to as a covenant in 2 Sam 23:5), and his reign will be viewed as the high point in the history of Israel. However, he is also presented in the narrative as one who would

---

65. One might also be tempted to include the poetic "last words of David," which would raise the count to three poetic texts. However, since the focus of this study is on *psalms* inserted into Hebrew narrative, I leave off the third text in this place.

66. It could be argued that David is the most important human figure in the Old Testament from the point of his first appearance in 1 Sam 16 onwards, as his name will appear 1,075 times in the Hebrew Bible and the time of his reign will be looked upon as the high point in the history of God's people. Also note that while Watts presents the material in 1 and 2 Samuel as a redactional unity, I am simply working with the final form as an integrative whole, without comment on the text's prehistory. For a more in-depth discussion of these two inset psalms in the context of 1 and 2 Samuel, see Watts, *Psalm and Story*, 19–40, 99–117.

67. While Watts notes the proleptic nature of this psalm in the books of Samuel, he does not list the horn as one of his links with the narrative that follows. See Watts, *Psalm and Story*, 22–24.

have chosen to incur bloodguilt had YHWH not saved him from it (1 Sam 25:22ff), as a polygamist who fails to heed the warning to not take many wives (1 Sam 25:42–44; cf. Deut 17:17), and as an adulterer and murderer who needed to be induced to repentance through prophetic rebuke (2 Sam 11–12), even before the failure of the census (and subsequent repentance) at the end of 2 Samuel (ch. 24). In other words, David is presented in narrative texts as a flawed but forgiven and faithful king over the people of God, even as poetic texts near the bookends of the narrative will anticipate his greatness (1 Sam 2) and record his pious words of thanksgiving (2 Sam 22). Further to this, in the New Testament the Christ will be presented as the Son of David (cf. 2 Sam.7), but this should be no surprise, for this is how the later Old Testament texts also anticipated him.[68] Evidently David's failures did not change YHWH's commitment to him or his use as an instrument of YHWH and type of the Messiah. His presentation in narrative and poetry were not seen as disruptive to those who shaped the final form of 1 and 2 Samuel, then, but as two integrative sides of a rounded presentation of this complex figure.

A second complicated figure whose presentation in a Hebrew narrative text does not contain poetic texts is the person of Abraham. In the Genesis narrative, this "father of the faithful" could in one instance believe God and have this credited to him as righteousness (Gen 15:6), and in the next chapter not believe God and marry his wife's slave girl (Gen 16). Further, Abraham could also, as a pattern over the course of his adult life, claim that his wife was his sister out of fear of being murdered (cf. Gen 20:13)! This is but one additional example of a faithful worshiper of YHWH who, *after* some of his great acts of faith, was also shown to be a horrible failure. And yet within the Christian canon Abraham is mentioned in "the great faith hall of fame" in Hebrews 11. Evidently, in the Genesis narrative his later failures did not change YHWH's commitment to him or the usefulness of his model acts of piety for later believers in Jesus.

In conclusion, then, as it was with David and Abraham, so it was with Jonah, a conflicted prophet, yes, but also one who would, within the Christian canon, be set forth as a type of Christ, in both his three days in the tomb,[69] and in his successful preaching ministry (cf. Matt 12:39–41;

---

68. Cf. among many other texts, Ps 2.

69. Note that 1 Pet 3:18ff indicates that for Christ the grave was not a place of defeat but a time when he preached to spirits in prison. This would coincide with the interpretation of Jonah's time in the belly of the fish as a time of salvation/rescue, and confirms the consistency of the type/antitype between Jonah and the Gospels.

16:4; Luke 11:29–32). To borrow some terms from systematic theology, would it not be possible that Jonah was genuinely repentant and further along on the sanctification trajectory after his rescue at sea, but shown two chapters later to be not wholly sanctified and in need of further correction from YHWH as the remaining sin of his heart was displayed? Far from evincing a disruptive interpolation, then, the conflicted prophet between psalm and narrative in Jonah offers a powerful display of God's covenant grace to the conflicted reader of the book of Jonah.

Concluding Remarks

Although the psalm of Jonah in its narrative context has proved a challenge for interpreters, the difficult work is to be rewarded. The book of Jonah and the Book of the Twelve would not be the same without this pious prayer that is certainly integrative in the context of the book as a whole. The poem's inclusion makes sense in light of considerations concerning vocabulary and the art of inserting poetry into Hebrew prose. Its inclusion adds interpretive value in light of the ironic/parabolic nature of the book of Jonah and the book in the context of the Twelve. Finally, the pious prayer provides lessons about the earthy, imperfect walk of faith that all of God's people experience.

Zerubbabel, Persia, and Inner-biblical Exegesis

DAVID B. SCHREINER

Indiana Wesleyan University,
College of Adult Professional Studies
dbschreiner@gmail.com

This essay discusses the socio-political expectations surrounding Zerubbabel as disclosed in Hag 2:20–23. Concurring with the consensus that Jer 22:24–30 is critical to understanding Hag 2:20–23, this essay engages the ideas of Wolter Rose and John Kessler, ultimately concluding that Hag 2:20–23 embodies a manto-typological exegesis of the Jeremianic tradition. Thus, Haggai is communicating to Zerubbabel that his role moving forward corresponds to his Davidic predecessors but is not tantamount to it. By implication, the prophet is proclaiming that the Davidic line will continue to play a role for the Second Temple community.

KEYWORDS: *Zerubbabel, Persia, Haggai, Inner-biblical Exegesis, Davidic Dynasty*

INTRODUCTION

Zerubbabel in his historical context is one of the most mysterious and thought-provoking situations in all of the Old Testament. In "The Mysterious Disappearance of Zerubbabel," Ted Lewis surveys the political landscape of early Persian Period Judah in order to determine what can be deduced from Zerubbabel's appearance and then abrupt disappearance.[1] He ultimately concludes, based on the investigative principle of who-stands-to-benefit-the-most-by-Zerubbabel's-disappearance, that the priesthood was most likely involved in his disappearance.[2] By

---

[1]. Theodore J. Lewis, "The Mysterious Disappearance of Zerubbabel," in *Seeking Out the Wisdom of the Ancients: Essays Offered to Honor Michael V. Fox on the Ocassion of His Sixty-Fifth Birthday* (ed. Ronald L. Troxel, Kelvin G. Friebel, and Dennis R. Magary; Winona Lake, IN: Eisenbrauns, 2005), 301–14.

[2]. Lewis, "The Mysterious Disappearance of Zerubbabel," 313–14.

implication, one gains the impression that early Persian period Judah was the center of ambition and political subterfuge, all of which was brought to a head with the events of Dairus I's initial years on the Persian throne. However, and to his credit, Lewis tempers his intriguing con-clusions when he states, "Ultimately, this is a mystery that we cannot solve."[3]

Zerubbabel's abrupt disappearance from the biblical and historical record is an intriguing case. However, this essay will engage Zerubbabel's mysteriousness from a different angle as it will attempt to understand some of the expectations surrounding his service to the Second Temple community. Focus will fall upon Hag 2:20–23, the critical passage for any attempt to understand Zerubbabel's socio-political role. Indeed, Hag 2:20–23 has not suffered from a dearth of commentary, and so after sketching the briefest of pictures, contributions by Walter Rose and John Kessler will be discussed in detail as their ideas offer an intriguing way forward. Yet this essay will reframe Kessler's work by discussing the strategic use of the כ prefix in terms of inner-biblical exegesis. This essay proposes that Hag 2:20–23 is a manto-typological exegesis of the tradition of Jer 22:24–30,[4] disclosing that Zerubbabel's socio-political role will be akin but not tantamount to his Davidic predecessors. Thus, the Davidic dynasty represents a viable socio-political option moving forward.

---

3. Ibid., 305.

4. The scholarly consensus recognizes that the sense of Jer 22:24–30 is the necessary cognitive backdrop for understanding the full implications of the Haggai oracle. For views representative of the debate's poles, see William Holladay, *Jeremiah* (Hermeneia; 2 vols.; Minneapolis, MN: Ausburg Fortress, 1986–90), 1:608–09; William McKane, *Jeremiah* (ICC; 2 vols.; Edinburgh: T&T Clark, 1986), 1:546–52.). Most germane is the status of Jer 22:24 within the debate. Even those who argue for a complicated textual history of the Jeremianic text often concede that v. 24 with its signet imagery is likely the earliest ele-ment. For example, McKane (*Jeremiah*, 1:544) understands v. 24 to be the "nucleus" that was subject to expansion. Consequently, understanding v. 24 as a foundational element to the Jeremianic pericope virtually ensures that Haggai, Zerubbabel, and the early Second Temple community would have been aware of the tradition that decried judgment upon Jehoiachin and, by implication, his progeny. Indeed, the status of v. 30 with its explicit rejection of Jehoiachin's progeny does not enjoy the benefit of a scholarly consensus. However, whether or not v. 30 was later inserted into the original oracle is a moot point, at least for the present task. Haggai invokes חותם. Such an invocation directly correlates the person of Zerubbabel with Jehoiachin, which is critical to understanding the type of inner-biblical exegesis (see below). Furthermore, the rejection of one's descendents from the right to rule is the logical implication of the rejection of the Davidic monarch.

Framing the Debate

The range of opinions regarding what Hag 2:20–23 says about the role of Zerubbabel and the Davidic dynasty can be broadly demarcated. Does Haggai foresee an imminent role for Zerubbabel and the Davidic line or one that is more distant and/or abstract? In the case of the former, scholars who understand Hag 2:20–23 either as a call for insurrection against Darius I and Persia or as an expectation of Persia's fall often find their greatest support in 1) the socio-political milieu of the first years of Darius I's reign and 2) a particular pericope in First Zechariah.[5] For example, Leroy Waterman advocated that Haggai's final oracle in conjunction with his temple-centric vision "culminate in the confident expectation of freedom from Persian rule and the immediate establishment of an independent Jewish state."[6] According to Waterman, the proof exists in the masoretic tradition's reading of Zech 6:9–14, which softens the prophetic words in an attempt "to hide from view the pitiable spectacle of two loyal and devoted prophets and a worthy governor of the royal line of David who unwittingly and solely because of inefficient means of communication were thus pilloried before the larger world and liquidated as craven conspirators."[7]

While Waterman's argument has been systematically critiqued,[8] Rainer Albertz and Joseph Blenkinsopp represent more recent conclusions that emphasize the value of Darius I's turbulent socio-political context in understanding Haggai's vision for Zerubbabel and the Davidic line. Hypothesizing the need for Darius to secure his southwestern border, Albertz suggests that the establishment of Zerubbabel as governor was an attempt to appeal to the nationalistic senses of the Judeans and secure fidelity. However, Darius's gamble must have failed for Albertz understands Zech 6:9–14 as substantiation that Zerubbabel was removed from the scene.[9] More pointedly than Albertz, Blenkinsopp sees

---

5. On the undeniable theological continuity between Haggai and First Zechariah, which may also be indicative of compositional continuity, see Eric M. Meyers and Carol L. Meyers, *Haggai, Zechariah 1–8* (AB 25B; Garden City, NJ: DoubleDay, 1987).

6. Leroy Waterman, "The Camouflaged Purge of Three Messianic Conspirators," *JNES* 13 (1954): 76.

7. Waterman, "The Camoflaged Purge," 78.

8. Peter Ackroyd, "Two Old Testament Historical Problems of the Early Persian Period," *JNES* 17 (1958): 13–27.

9. Rainer Albertz, *Israel In Exile: The History and Literature of the Sixth Century B.C.E.* (trans. David Green; Atlanta, GA: SBL, 2003), 125–26.

Haggai's final oracle as "the prediction of the overthrow of the Persian Empire and the restoration of the native dynasty," which is supported vividly via the חותם imagery.[10] The language according to Blenkinsopp is indicative of a "messianic movement in Judah, comparable with the movement in contemporary Babylon, triggered by the political turmoil throughout the Persian Empire between the death of Cambyses in July 522 and the final restoration of order by Darius two years later."[11]

While the views of Waterman, Albertz, and Blenkinsopp correctly emphasize not only the Persian method of governance that utilized indigenous dynasties[12] but also the effects of the turbulent socio-political milieu upon the interpretation of Haggai's final words to Zerubbabel, points of criticism can be leveled against such types of interpretive positions. First, there is an assumption that the people of Judah exhibited the same attitude and/or actions of rebellion as those in other parts of the empire. Yet as Sarah Japhet states, "The data available to us at this stage do not enable us to reconstruct such a rebellion in Israel's history."[13] Indeed, one may point to Zech 6:9–14 as evidence, which has been the case. However, not only is this evidence circumstantial at best, but if one sees Zech 6:9–14 as an intentional emendation, then one must consider other textual issues that, according to Eric and Carol Meyers, do more harm than good.[14] Finally, interpretive positions that perceive Haggai's final words to Zerubbabel as a call for insurrection and/or the anticipation of an immediate restoration of the Davidic line do not properly consider the following phenomena: 1) the full implications of the phrase ביום ההוא; 2) the association of Hag 2:20–23 with Hag 2:6–9 and the implications that follow, and 3) the cosmic battle motif in Hag 2:20–23. All of these phenomena converge to suggest an eschatologicalization occurring within the oracle, which in turn implies that the prophet may have been recalibrating the audience's perspective toward the future and less on immediate insurrection and restoration of the Davidic dynasty

---

10. Joseph Blenkinsopp, *A History of Prophecy in Israel* (rev. and en. ed.; Louisville: Westminster John Knox, 1996), 202–03.

11. Ibid., 203.

12. André Lemaire, "Zorobabel Et La Judée À La Lumière De L'Épigraphie (Fin Du VIe S. AV. J.–C.)," *RB* 103 (1996): 48–57.

13. Sara Japhet, "Sheshbazzar and Zerubbabel against the Background of the Historical and Religious Tendencies of Ezra-Nehemiah," *ZAW* 94 (1982): 24.

14. Meyers and Meyers, *Haggai, Zechariah 1–8*, 350–53.

under Zerubbabel.[15] Many scholars emphasize the eschatological nuances of this oracle and thus understand the function of Zerubbabel and the Davidic dynasty spoken of in this oracle as indicative of something that will enjoy its maturation in another dispensation.

For example, Pieter Verhoef acknowledges how "the recent upheaval among the warring nations would have contributed to this imagery,"[16] but the eschatological nuances of the oracle are too great to be ignored. Thus, according to Verhof, Haggai's final words suggest "a wider perspective than the person of the Judean governor as the contemporary of the prophet."[17] Meyers and Meyers also understand the eschatological nuances of the oracle to be quite pervasive. For example, they believe Hag 2:20–23 to be the "inevitable conclusion to 2:15–19," which deals with future realities. Second, the Hiphil forms of רעש and הפך with the phrase ביום ההוא import a distinctly eschatological flavor. Meyers and Meyers also understand the imagery surrounding the function of Zerubbabel to display "instrumentability" and "vice-regency."[18] Thus, "The overwhelming imagery of the oracle is not only eschatology, it is also theocratic."[19]

The conclusions of Verhoef and Meyers and Meyers are representative of those that correctly emphasize an important characteristic of Haggai's final oracle—its eye for the future. In other words, Haggai appears to envision a dispensation that exists beyond the present socio-political context. Therefore, when this reality is considered alongside the socio-political characteristics of the second year of Darius I, a dialectic appears in this oracle as it relates to the expectations of Zerubbabel and the Davidic dynasty. The function of neither Zerubbabel nor the Davidic line can be understood solely by concrete and immediate realities or solely by those that are more distant and more abstract.

---

15. Thus, I am invoking the terms "eschatologicalization" and "eschatology" generically, broadly referring "to Israel's orientation toward the future as the arena where God will act decisively in accord with God's deity, promises, and commands." See R. Kendall Soulen and Richard N. Soulen, "Eschatology," in *Handbook of Biblical Criticism* (3d ed.; Louisville, KY: Westminster John Knox, 2001), 55.

16. Pieter A. Verhoef, *Haggai and Malachi* (NICOT; Grand Rapids, MI: Eerdmans, 1987), 140.

17. Ibid., 150.

18. Meyers and Meyers, *Haggai, Zechariah 1–8*, 68.

19. Ibid., 47.

ROSE, KESSLER, AND A WAY FORWARD

Walter Rose has provided an important discussion on the expectations associated with Zerubbabel and by implication the Davidic line.[20] Appearing at the end of his lengthy and intricate discussion of Zerubbabel, Rose emphasizes key phrases detailed in Hag 2:20–23. Zerubbabel is called a "servant" (עבד), he is "chosen" (בחר) and "taken" (לקח), and is to be made like a חותם. In the case of the first three phrases, Rose rightly argues that while each is associated with the Davidic traditions, the nuances of the Haggai context militate against any simplistic assumption that Zerubbabel is being perceived as another royal figure in the vein of his forefather David. עבד is associated with David on numerous occasions, but only rarely with others.[21] בחר is associated only with the kings David and Saul,[22] and the invocation of לקח to communicate a divinely sanctioned mission restricts the semantic possibilities.[23] Ultimately, Rose emphasizes that the marshalling of these terms to argue for royal expectations for Zerubbabel and the Davidic line overstates things.[24]

Rose's criticisms are valid to a certain point. On the one hand, his conclusions appear to disregard the logical principle of synergism—the whole is greater than the sum of its parts. Indeed, taken in isolation, neither of these terms demands that Zerubbabel enjoys royal expectations, but when considered together in the context of the early Persian period along with Zerubbabel's Davidic lineage, it seems only logical that the expectations pertaining to Zerubbabel will inform the "royal" prerogatives of the dynastic line moving forward.[25] In other words, Rose's desire to expose the semantic possibilities on his way to separating the passage from Davidic undertones ultimately creates a dubious dynamic. On the other hand, Rose is correct to suggest that there are subtle nuances in the terms and images used, and they converge to reveal

---

20. Wolter H. Rose, *Zemah and Zerubbabel: Messianic Expectations in the Early Postexilic Period* (JSOTSup 304; Sheffield: Sheffield Academic, 2000).

21. Ibid., 211.

22. Ibid., 213–16.

23. Ibid., 218.

24. Ibid., 210–18.

25. I use the parenthesis around the term "royal" intentionally. As will be detailed, I think that the prophet is addressing the royal expectations of Zerubbabel and the Davidic line. However, the subtleties of the prophet's message suggest that any royal expectation should be nuanced.

the prophet's intention. These revelations are furthered upon considering the phrase ושמתיך כחותם (v. 23).

It is critical to understand that Rose perceives Jer 22:24 to be the context necessary to properly Haggai's intentions in this phrase. "[Jer 22:24] is generally seen as in some way providing the background to the verse in Haggai, and I think this observation is valid."[26] Also, "I do not want to disagree with finding a connection between two oracles . . ."[27] But what separates Rose from many interpreters is his assertion that Jeremiah is declaring that Jehoiachin has no personal worth in the eyes of the Lord (versus the rejection of him as a royal authority). While lengthy, Rose's argument clues on the syntax of the Jeremianic context and the usage of the generic term חותם (versus the more specific term טבעת). Moreover, Rose states that just because the immediate context of the Jeremianic oracle is royal in its agenda, it does not necessarily follow that all the oracles speak to kingship. Ultimately, the imagery invoked by Jeremiah in 22:24 is not what is expected when a signet ring that represents authority is cast off. Thus, "[King Jehoiachin] is compared to a seal on the hand of Yhwh, symbol of high personal value, but he has lost his privileged position, and Yhwh feels like throwing him away, as if he had become an objection of no personal value at all."[28]

With respect to the effect these conclusions have on Hag 2:23, Rose stresses the similarity between passages, namely that the imagery invoked by Haggai is not consistent with the declaration of royal authority by means of a signet ring. The Lord gives nothing to Zerubbabel. Rather, the Lord's desire is to make him like a חותם.[29] Important for Rose is the use of a simile.[30] As for the socio-political upheaval anticipated in vv. 20–23, no explicit statements exist that demand a nuance of royal authority.[31] "One does not find a statement about Zerubbabel being Yhwh's anointed or about his autonomous rule (governed by God) present or future, and there is no explicit promise that God will make the

---

26. Rose, *Zemah and Zerubbabel*, 221–22.

27. Ibid., 235.

28. Ibid., 228–29.

29. Ibid., 237–38.

30. Ibid., 238. Rose emphasizes the כ preposition. See below for other implications associated with this prefix.

31. Ibid., 241–42.

nations subject to his chosen one."³² In the end, Rose perceives there to be an expectation that Zerubbabel will experience the opposite of his ancestor. He will enjoy personal worth or value in the eyes of the Lord.

Rose's argument does well to stress that Jer 22:24 is the cognitive backdrop necessary for understanding the prophetic declaration to Zerubbabel. Furthermore, he correctly highlights the nuances of the imagery and language and draws laudable interpretive conclusions. However, the vagaries of the oracle may not necessarily be indicative of what he characterizes simply as a non-royal expectation. It could be that something more nuanced is involved. To flesh out this point, John Kessler's article "Haggai, Zerubbabel, and the Political Status of Yehud: The Signet Ring in Haggai 2:23" becomes important.³³

According to Kessler, understanding the expectations surrounding Zerubbabel and the Davidic dynasty initially requires the consideration of four issues. The first is the political status of Judah. The debate regarding this topic is fierce, but Kessler categorizes four options.³⁴ First, Judah was a part of the province of Samaria. Second, Judah briefly enjoyed status as an independent province, but was quickly consumed by the province of Samaria. Third, Judah enjoyed a lengthy period of independence and was governed by a relatively stable line of Jewish governors. Fourth, Judah was a vassal-kingdom during the Babylonian and Early Persian periods and was ruled by a member of the Davidic dynasty. Kessler sides with option three, based on biblical, lexical, and archaeological data. The second issue to consider is the association of Hag 2:21–23 with 2:6–9. According to Kessler, both passages "use language of present acceptability despite inferior status."³⁵ Third, one must consider Haggai's hermeneutics of generalization. Kessler believes that Haggai intentionally generalizes, attenuates, and obfuscates popular prophetic motifs in order to focus the audience's attention upon the most salient elements.³⁶ Fourth, the nature and purpose of the signet ring imagery in Jer 22:24 and Hag 2:23 is critical, and

---

32. Ibid., 240–41.

33. John Kessler, "Haggai, Zerubbabel, and the Political Status of Yehud: The Signet Ring in Haggai 2:23," in *Prophets, Prophecy, and Prophetic Texts in Second Temple Judaism* (ed. Michael Floyd and Robert D. Haak; LBHOTS 427; New York: T&T Clark, 2006), 102–19.

34. Ibid., 103–06.

35. Ibid., 107.

36. In the case of Hag 2:23, the most salient point is the realization that "Zerubbabel will experience exaltation at the hand of Yahweh." Ibid., 110.

Kessler believes that two realizations illuminate this nexus most clearly. On the one hand, the use of חותם is intentional as it functions to update Jer 22:24 in light of the circumstances of the early Persian period, and on the other hand, the issue at stake is the personification of Yahweh. The חותם imagery is a means to an end. According to Kessler therefore,

> The real trope consists of the personification of Yahweh, who is likened to the owner of a signet who, in one case, in utter anger and disgust, despite its preciousness to him, removes his signet and throws it away, and who, in the other, due to changed circumstances, picks up that which was formerly discarded and puts it on again.[37]

Armed with these principles, Kessler argues that Haggai's final oracle is intentionally vague in its address to the function of Zerubbabel and the Davidic dynasty. On the one hand, it is clear that Haggai responds to the oracle of Jeremiah by stating that that which was pronounced in Jeremiah is undone. On the other hand, Haggai is intentionally unclear about the details. "What is lacking, however, in the text of Haggai . . . is an indication of *the precise nature* of the correspondingly positive future experience of Zerubbabel."[38] Thus, Kessler believes that this final oracle tempers any misplaced nationalism as it encourages the community to "accept the then-present realities" as evidence that "Yahweh's promises to the nation and its royal house were not defunct."[39]

There is much with which to agree in Kessler's article. He properly considers the socio-historical context behind Hag 2:20–23, including an awareness of Persian political policy and the era of insurrection, without compromising the demands of the text. Of those demands, Kessler properly weighs the eschatological nuances, which allows him to conclude that the prophet has one eye fixed on the future. However, in the remainder of this essay I will reframe particular elements of Kessler's presentation, namely his statements that Hag 2:23 "corrects" Jer 22:24 and the nuances of the כ preposition prefixed to חותם. A consideration of inner-biblical exegesis offers an illuminating perspective that explains the now-future dialectic, the nuanced imagery

---

37. Ibid., 113.

38. Ibid., 115.

39. Ibid., 117.

associated with חותם, and the convergence of literary traditions in a Second Temple context.

INNER-BIBLICAL EXEGESIS: REFRAMING KESSLER

It is incontrovertible that the phrase כחותם is a *crux* for Hag 2:20–23 and its expectations of Zerubbabel and the Davidic line's role moving forward. As for the significance of this phrase, the implications of inner-biblical exegesis offer an intriguing explanation. According to Fishbane, certain socio-religious and historical developments engendered the reinterpretation and contextualization of authoritative traditions, and the vestiges of this process can be detected within the biblical tradition. Fishbane has proposed four basic types of inner-biblical exegesis: scribal, legal, aggadic, and mantological. What concerns this essay initially is mantological exegesis, which considers that which is "ominous or oracular in scope."[40] Moreover, mantological exegesis may be visual or auditory, transformative or non-transformative. Thus, Hag 2:20–23 can be understood as a type of transformative mantological exegesis of the Jeremianic tradition that "readapts, reapplies, or revises" the older oracle.[41] More specifically, it mitigates the cognitive dissonance[42] that was undoubtedly present amongst the people of early Persian period Judah. Having experienced the Babylonian exile, and the fulfillment of Jeremiah's denouncement of Jehoiachin, the presence of a Davidic heir in one of the highest profile political positions in conjunction with the political upheaval of Darius's second year would have imported confusion, wonder, and uncertainty.

Interestingly, Kessler describes these dynamics but falls short of using terms familiar to inner-biblical exegesis. Consider a somewhat lengthy statement.

---

40. Michael Fishbane, *Biblical Interpretation in Ancient Israel* (Oxford: Clarendon, 1985), 443.

41. Ibid., 460. On how the idea of readapting, reapplying, or revising the prophetic word interacts with a view of scriptural inspiration, see below.

42. Ibid., 445. On cognitive dissonance and biblical prophecy, see Robert P. Carroll, *When Prophecy Failed: Cognitive Dissonance in the Prophetic Traditions of the Old Testament* (New York: Seabury, 1979); idem, "Ancient Israelite Prophecy and Dissonance Theory," in *The Place is Too Small for Us: The Israelite Prophets in Recent Scholarship* (ed. R. P. Gordon; Winona Lake, IN: Eisenbrauns, 1995), 377–91; reprint *Numen* 24 (1977): 135–51.

[T]he use of the signet imagery was not one option out of a vast range of possibilities. Rather it was taken up specifically because of its presence in the Jeremianic tradition. In all probability, the tradition cried out for further reflection once the Davidic Zerubbabel was reinstated by the Persians. How did the presence of Zerubbabel square with Jeremiah's words of rejection directed against Jehoiachin and his descendents? How could those who treasured those words—possibly the non-exiled community, as opposed to the returnees—follow the leadership of Zerubbabel (a member of the returnee group) in the temple reconstruction project? The critical interpretive questions vis-à-vis Hag 2:23 is thus not "How is Zerubbabel like a signet ring?" but rather "How does Hag 2:23 develop the ideas of Jer 22:24–30?[43]

From this quote, one sees that Kessler recognizes that the hermeneutical connection between the two passages is such that Haggai's oracle addresses the authoritative tradition in order to alleviate the confusion that would have arisen in light of present circumstances.

Yet, there appears to be another level to this prophetic exegesis, and to unpack this, the prefixed כ becomes the point of focus as it can signal inner-biblical exegesis. More specifically, it may signal typological inner-biblical exegesis, a specific type of aggadic exegesis.[44] According to Fishbane, typology "sees in previous events or places the prototype pattern, or figure of historical persons, events or places that follow it in time."[45] Inner-biblical typologies therefore "constitute a literary-historical phenomenon which isolates perceived correlations between specific events, persons, or places in time with their later correspondents"[46] As to the nature of the relationship between correspondents, Fishbane states,

[The later correspondents] will never be precisely identical with

---

43. Kessler, "Haggai, Zerubbabel, and Yehud," 112–13.

44. According to Fishbane, "fixed rhetorical terms" signal typological exegesis, and in such cases כאשר . . . כן is frequent. However, Fishbane admits, "Now and then כאשר is replaced by כ- and variants." Fishbane, *Biblical Interpretation*, 352. Other scholars recognize the role of the כ prefix in signaling inner-biblical exegesis (e.g., Bruce K. Waltke and M. O'Connor, *An Introduction to Biblical Hebrew Syntax* [Winona Lake, IN: Eisenbrauns, 1990], 202–05).

45. Fishbane, *Biblical Interpretation*, 351.

46. Ibid., 351.

their prototype, but inevitably stand in hermeneutical relationship with them. Not only do typologies emphasize the likeness between two correspondents, but the nexus between them is always exegetically established.[47]

Applied to Hag 2:20–23, this oracle also appears to be a typology of a biographical nature. By invoking terms and ideology traditionally associated with the Davidic dynasty alongside the חותם imagery, which was particularly significant for Zerubbabel's grandfather Jehoiachin, the prophet is defining Zerubbabel's role, and the Davidic dynasty which he represents, through a correlation with the Davidic descendent who was ushered off to Babylon and signified the rejection of that line. Thus, Zerubbabel can be perceived in one sense as the anti-Jehoiachin, signifying that the Davidic line will once again play a strategic role for the Second Temple community. Yet one would be incorrect to insist that Zerubbabel's role will correspond exactly to the roles of his preexilic predecessors. As this essay has discussed, there are methodological, historical, and interpretive factors that work against such a conclusion. Instead, the prophet is espousing that Zerubbabel's role will correspond to that of his forefathers' as king but not be tantamount to it. With Zerubbabel, the Davidic dynasty will again enjoy the position of the community's figurehead and highest-ranking political official. In other words, Zerubbabel symbolizes that the Davidic dynasty represents a viable political option moving forward, albeit in a nuanced fashion. By implication, Haggai is communicating that the Davidic covenant is not null and void.

Conclusion

In sum, this essay has discussed in detail the conclusions of Walter Rose and John Kessler on the expectations surrounding Zerubbabel, and by implication the Davidic line, according to Hag 2:20–23. While Rose offers some important considerations—that Jer 22:24 is the necessary cognitive backdrop and that the imagery of both Jer 22:24 and Hag 2:23 is nuanced—this essay suggests that John Kessler best understands the host of dynamics involved with trying to ascertain the expectations of Zerubbabel and the Davidic dynasty. Kessler best considers the socio-political dynamics of the second year of Darius I, the Persian use of indigenous dynasties to ensure political stability, and the imagery and content of Haggai's final oracle in its immediate and book-level contexts.

---

47. Ibid., 351.

Most importantly, Kessler properly explains that the hermeneutical relationship between Jer 22:24 and Hag 2:23 is paramount when trying to understand the expectations surrounding the Davidic line. Yet this essay also reframed Kessler's work in terms of inner-biblical exegesis. This essay suggests that Hag 2:20–23 constitutes a complex manto-typological exegesis of the Jer 22:24–30 tradition.[48] On the one hand, it clarified the dissonance that would have existed within the Second Temple community as it tried to rectify the Jeremianic tradition with the realities of the second year of Darius I (mantological exegesis). On the other hand, it communicated that Zerubbabel's socio-political role could be correlated with those of his monarchic predecessors, but just not in the exact same capacity (typological exegesis). By implication, Haggai's final oracle also communicated that the Davidic line would enjoy political viability and continued divine sanction as the future unfolded, even if in a nuanced way.

But does Hag 2:20–23 constitute a "reversal" of the Jermianic tradition? Rose is hesitant. "I do not want to disagree with finding a connection between the two oracles, though I would be somewhat cautious about whether one can say that Haggai was consciously reversing the Jeremiah oracle."[49] Yet in light of the proposal offered here, one must concede that the Haggai oracle *reverses* the Jeremianic one, at least in a general sense. The debate of whether חותם conveys a sense of authority or personal value notwithstanding, that which was done in Jehoiachin is undone—or reversed—in the person of Zerubbabel.

Assuming this concession, another more fundamental question particularly relevant for evangelicals creeps to the forefront. Does such a concession erode one's view of scriptural inspiration? Does conceding a reversal of the prophetic word undermine a high view of Scripture? According to Lawson Stone, the final form of Scripture is the "apex" of a lengthy process of textual development that saw Israel's authoritative traditions pass through various stages of growth and transmission.[50] By implication, "all stages of development are regarded as participating to

---

48. Admittedly, such a complex exegesis may be unique. However, as argued, both typological and mantological types are present. Yet more fundamentally, the proposal offered here embodies the essence of inner-biblical exegesis. As emphasized by Fishbane, there is a vibrant and protean relationship between the traditio and traditum. To restrict it by any preconceived notion undermines the exegetical activity. See Fishbane, *Biblical Interpretation*, 13.

49. Rose, *Zemah and Zerubbabel*, 235.

50. Lawson G. Stone, "On Historical Authenticity, Historical Criticism, and Biblical Authority: Reflections on the Case of the Book of Joshua," *AsTJ* 56/57 (2002): 85.

some degree in divine revelation and inspiration. Development is not inimical to the truth-value of Scripture. The progressive development of Scripture has a role in the overall picture of God's historical revelation."[51] Therefore, inspiration is not static and merely a feature of the text's final form. It is dynamic and a divinely sanctioned influence that oversaw the entire process of the canon's formation.

Haggai's reversal of the Jeremianic tradition therefore should not be understood negatively. Rather, the textual relationship described in this essay provides a window into the progressive nature of God's revelation. It demonstrates how God's word continually nourished the community by explaining their experiences and, when necessary, revisiting past experiences in light of newly disclosed prophetic insight that could clarify points of confusion. In this instance, the status of Zerubbabel in the early Second Temple period forced a reconsideration of an extant Jeremianic tradition. In the process, the Lord revealed through his prophet Haggai that redemption from exile was a reality that extended to persons and familial lines, not just nations.

---

51. Ibid., 85.

BOOK REVIEWS

Celebrate Her for the Fruit of Her Hands: Studies in Honor of Carol L. Meyers edited by Susan Ackerman, Charles E. Carter, and Beth Alpert Nakhai (with Karla G. Bohmbach and Franz Volker Greifenhagen). Winona Lake, IN: Eisenbrauns, 2015. xviii + 414 pp., US $59.50, hardcover.

This Festschrift for archaeologist and biblical scholar Carol Meyers of Duke University has been long in coming. The idea emerged with Charles E. Carter, a former student, in 2002–03, then invitations for contributors were sent out in 2006, then delays, but now in 2015 it finally emerges! The downside is that since nothing is cited as a source beyond 2008, the essays included are out of date. But the upside is that this is largely offset by the high quality of several of the essays. Contributions come from both Meyers's former students and colleagues. There are two encomia to Meyers that introduce the 19 essays: one from a former student (Carter) and one from a colleague (Susan Ackerman). There are indices of authors, Scripture, and other ancient sources. The methodologies of the essays include archaeological, feminist, sociological, anthropological, ideological, and theological, all tied together by a focus on social concerns, often gender, which is especially fitting for Meyers, who pioneered an anthropological and archaeological approach for highlighting the relatively high status of Israelite women. The title of the volume is also thereby fitting, coming from a verse (31) in the encomium to the noble woman in Prov 31:10–31—a favorite among feminists.

In "Hannah's Tears," Susan Ackerman (Dartmouth College) argues that in 1 Sam 1:9–18 Hannah's fasting and weeping before she approaches the Shiloh sanctuary are not signs of an emotionally distraught woman in dire straits but rather ritualistic acts meant to prod God to intervene on her behalf. In "Women, Law, and Legal Procedure in Ancient Israel," James P. Ashmore (Shaw University Divinity School) utilizes various ethnographic data in conjunction with relevant texts in the Hebrew Bible to argue that Israelite women appear to have had little role in the formal legal system and were at a clear disadvantage within it. In "Nationalist Narratives and Biblical Memory," Cynthia M. Baker (Bates College) traces how Zionists, the rabbis, and Palestinians have configured the land of Israel according to their own ideologies by selective remembering (e.g., Adam teaches Seth Torah), mapping (e.g.,

Arabic versus Hebrew toponyms), and embodying (e.g., hair styles). In "When It Both Is and Is Not Rape: Gender Constructions in 2 Samuel 13:1–22," former student Karla G. Bohmbach (Susquehanna University), while admitting that this passage may not technically be rape from the androcentric Israelite perspective, depicts Tamar as the quintessence of Israelite femininity (nubility, deception, and acquiescence), while Amnon displays androgyny. In "Speaking as 'Any Foolish Woman': Ms. Job in the History of Reception," Rhonda Burnette-Bletsch (Eastern University) traces the history of the treatment of Job's wife—usually negative but also neutral and positive—through textual traditions, commentaries, iconography, plays, and films, from ancient to modern times. The lack of photos of art work referenced in the essay is frustrating, especially in comparison with the essay by another contributor (Nakhai).

In "Numbers 5:11–31: Women in Second Temple Judah and the Law of the Controlling Priest," Claudia V. Camp (Texas Christian University) uses ideological criticism and ethnographic data to argue that the passage about the ordeal of the suspected adulteress involves the attempt of priestly power to appropriate not just women's role in biological and cultural reproduction (cultic roles) but also non-priestly males! In "'There Is Much Wisdom in Her': The Matriarchs in the Qumran Library," Sidnie White Crawford (University of Nebraska-Lincoln) surveys references to the Israelite matriarchs, including the handmaidens, in the Qumran library and finds that they are all shown to have impeccable genealogical credentials and that negative behavior recorded in the biblical text has often been expunged; correlatively, pure descent and piety were highly valued by the Qumran community. In "Poor but Wise (Qoheleth 9:13–16)," James Crenshaw (Duke University) explores the social location of the Teacher in view of his conception of God as *deus absconditus*. In "Reading the Bible as Agrarian Literature," Ellen F. Davis interprets Prov 31:10–31 from a theological and agrarian perspective and finds that the portrayal of the woman's wisdom as "situated knowledge" stands in contrast to imperial (Persian period) forms of wisdom. In "Israelite Women as 'Ritual Experts': Orthodoxy or Orthopraxis?" William G. Dever (the University of Arizona) ponders how archaeological evidence for Israelite women's cults can offset the androcentric bias of the male biblical authors, at least to a degree.

In "Structure and Origin of the Early Israelite and Iroquois Confederacies," Norman K. Gottwald (Pacific School of Religion) utilizes an ethnographic approach to argue for an Israelite confederacy in view of Martin Noth's faulty attempt to compare tribal Israel with the Greek amphictyony. In "The Place of Biblical Studies in the University Curriculum: Beyond the Religious/Secular Divide," former student Sandie

Gravett (Appalachian State University) attempts to offset the recent criticisms of the place of biblical studies within the academy (e.g., Jacques Berlinerblau and Hector Avalos) by suggesting an integration of it within a broader religious and cultural perspective that can still challenge truth claims. In "Bargaining with Patriarchy in the Book of Ruth," former student F. V. Greifenhagen (Luther College, University of Regina), utilizes the ethnographic notion of "patriarchal bargain" to explain the relationship between Naomi and Ruth, as mother- and daughter-in-law, that partially offsets their primary subordination to men.

In "Gendered Sectarians: Envisioning Women (and Men) at Qumran," former student Maxine L. Grossman (University of Maryland) surveys the statuses of men but especially women in the Qumran literature and reads against the grain by concluding that women were present in all the communities associated with Qumran, even that of the *Community Rule*. In "Translating Women: The Perils of Gender-Inclusive Translation of the New Testament," Ross S. Kraemer and Jennifer Eyl explore how the recent trend among biblical translators to use gender-inclusive language in fact has had unintended negative consequences for both the populace and scholars. In "Ethnicity, Culture, and Religion in Artifact and Text: The Emergence of Complex Common Judaism," spouse Eric M. Meyers (Duke University) builds on E. P. Sanders's term "common Judaism" to delineate how archaeologists can determine Jewish identity from artifacts. In "Plaque Figurines and the Relationship between Canaanite and Egyptian Women in the Late Bronze II," Beth Alpert Nakhai (the University of Arizona) examines two types of popular plaque figurines and speculates on how Egyptian and Canaanite women interacted in reproductive and ritual spheres.

In "The Story of David and Goliath from the Perspective of the Study of Oral Traditions," Raymond F. Person Jr. (Ohio Northern University) attempts to compare the MT and LXX versions of 1 Sam 16–18 with help from ethnographic data about oral traditions to argue that the two versions evidence the scribal tendency of preserving multiformity/fluidity of traditions. In "I Sing the Body Politic: Stillborn Desire and the Birth of Israel in Judges 5," former student Anathea Portier-Young (Duke University) exegetes the Song of Deborah, engaging both its redemptive (e.g., women's subjectivity) and irredeemable features (e.g., violence).

All in all, this is a significant volume. It is recommended for graduate courses and any biblical scholars interested in biblical sociology or anthropology.

MARK SNEED
Lubbock Christian University

2 Samuel by Robert Barron. Brazos Theological Commentary on the Bible. Edited by R. R. Reno. Grand Rapids, MI: Brazos, 2015. xxii + 219 pp., US $29.99, hardcover.

"Delightful" is rarely used, for a variety of reasons, to describe a biblical commentary, but it is an apt label for Robert Barron's *2 Samuel*. This addition to the Brazos Theological Commentary on the Bible Series is a volume that every pastor and Bible scholar should own and reference regularly. Not only will it assist the reader in understanding the particular chapters in 2 Samuel; it will also make them a more competent reader of the entire Bible, since virtually every page is filled with intertextual connections and narrative parallels between 2 Samuel and other parts of the Bible.

As with the rest of the Brazos Series, and almost every other commentary, Barron's volume follows the outline of the biblical book. Working with five "Series," or divisions of 2 Samuel, Barron navigates through individual chapters of 2 Samuel in each of his commentary's chapters. Series One details David's rise to power (2 Sam 1–2); Series Two covers David's "pre-fall" reign as Israel's priestly king (2 Sam 3–10); Series Three, on 2 Sam 11, exegetes the David and Bathsheba story; Series Four exposits the fracture of David's house (2 Sam 12–20); and Series Five covers the end of the book, anticipating Solomon's Temple building project (2 Sam 21–24).

2 Samuel is filled with intertextual threads, both biblical and extrabiblical, linking the chronicles of David's rise and fall to the scriptural canon, dogmatics, and various philosophies. The most compelling of these connections is the first; Barron's ability to *textually* tie David's story to those of Adam, Abraham, Moses, and, ultimately, Jesus, is astounding. Throughout the commentary the reader feels overwhelmed by the weight of biblical material pushing through each sentence of 2 Samuel and the textual-typological connections noted by Barron.

The most important of these, according to Barron, is the connection between David and Adam. The themes of kingship, wise rule, defeat of God's enemies, and dwelling with Yahweh in the land all narratively bond these two biblical figures, but Barron also shows that the author of 2 Samuel intends to textually tie them together through numerous allusions, echoes, and direct quotations of Gen 1–3 and other Adamic material. Barron also ably shows how this Adam-David connection is part and parcel of the biblical story, and, in part, the climax of Israel's story and her purpose of redeeming what Adam lost. Of course, neither David's story nor Israel's stops with 2 Sam 10, and so Barron also shows how David's decline in 2 Sam 11–24 is likewise typologically paradigmatic of Adam's, Solomon's, and Israel's failures. All of this points the reader forward to the fulfillment of God's redemptive purposes in Jesus Christ, as David serves as the type and Christ the antitype for YHWH's redeemer.

As with David, so with Barron's commentary, though; not all is as well as it seems. Of course, this reader's quibbles with Barron's work are inherently infinitesimal when compared with David's transgressions. Even so, there are a number of issues with Barron's commentary of which readers, and particularly evangelical readers, should be aware. First, Barron demonstrates a commitment to pacifism throughout the book. This is not a problem in and of itself (i.e., the quibble is not necessarily with that ethical position); the problem arises when this commitment to non-violence seems to strain the point of the text or the character of God as seen in the rest of Scripture. Second, Barron is writing as a Roman Catholic, and there are times when this comes through, namely his excurses on Thomistic thought. On the whole, though, when compared with other Catholic commentaries, Barron's is fairly tame with respect to showing his confessional cards and so the evangelical reader should not be overly distracted by the minimal references to them. Finally, it is unclear where Barron stands on historical-critical issues. While the Brazos Series intentionally focuses on theological readings, the quickness with which Barron slides past these important matters can be vexing for readers of all stripes.

In spite of these relatively minor quibbles, *2 Samuel* is highly recommended for its textual insights, theological depth, and literary skill. Barron's adeptness in weaving together intertextual links, narrative parallels, typology, philosophy, and classic Christian theology make this commentary a rich tapestry filled with insight and erudition. It should be on the shelf of every student of Scripture.

MATTHEW Y. EMERSON
Oklahoma Baptist University

For the Glory of God: Recovering a Biblical Theology of Worship by Daniel I. Block. Grand Rapids, MI: Baker Academic, 2014, vii + 410 pp., US $34.99, hardcover.

Daniel I. Block, Professor of Old Testament at Wheaton College, writes from the conviction that "true worship involves reverential human acts of submission and homage before the divine Sovereign in response to his gracious revelation of himself and in accord with his will" (p. 23). Block seeks to elucidate this thesis by synthesizing all that the Bible says concerning the topic of worship. What Block ultimately seeks to "recover" as the title suggests, is a theology of worship that takes into account the actual words of the Bible, a theology that derives from deep reflection on the Bible and which concerns all of life, not simply the Sunday service.

The book is driven by two foundational principles. First, "true worship is essentially a vertical exercise, the human response to the divine Creator and Redeemer" (p. 6). Block reiterates this point at the beginning of every chapter. Since worship is vertical, its aim is directed to the glory of God instead of the pleasure of human beings, a notion that is lost in the contemporary worship scene today.

The second foundational principle is that "knowledge of nature and forms of worship that glorify God comes primarily from Scripture" (p. 6). Thus, the Old Testament (OT, or "First Testament" as Block has a penchant for saying) and New Testament (NT) are the rule of worship. All forms and practices must derive from them. Being a professor of OT for several decades, Block makes his case primarily from that section of the Bible, and particularly from the Pentateuch. Indeed, he states, "since the NT gives minimal attention to corporate worship, true Christian worship should be grounded on theological principles established in the First Testament" (p. 25).

Block contends that a recovery of biblical worship must begin with definitions. Indeed, every chapter is full of them, which in Block's style is not boring but engaging. After addressing the object and subjects of worship in the Bible (Christ and Christians, respectively), the first half of the book deals with daily work and family life as worship. The second half addresses a series of topics more naturally associated with worship: liturgical exercises practiced by the assembled community of faith such as ordinances, preaching, prayer, music, sacrifice/offerings, and leadership.

Block concludes his work with several appendices, including a chart of all doxologies in the Bible, the "Hymnic Fragments in the Pauline Epistles," and translations of source documents of "Sunday Worship in Early Christianity." Block also has a fondness for diagrams, which are provided throughout the book and very helpful considering the scope of this project, although some of these diagrams are useless (see Figure 6.3, "The Eucharistic Helix," p. 158).

A large-scale publication on biblical worship is needed for every generation, and Block has provided it for this one. The amount of detail and careful exegesis in every chapter is unparalleled among books on this topic. *For the Glory of God* is thus an excellent sourcebook but could also serve as a manual for conducting church worship since Block seeks primarily to be faithful to the biblical text.

Block is right to note that Christians have wiped away the significance of the OT in worship, a key theme of this book. Christians often operate under a practical Marcionism that is foreign to what Jesus and the apostles commended the church to do, and many times their only appeal to worship in the OT is to the book of Psalms. Block admonishes Christians who dismiss the OT as irrelevant for establishing a theology and practice of worship, or those who do so solely from the Psalms. This is a helpful corrective, and a return to the OT for establishing the principles of worship in the NT is part of the "recovery" process as well. Indeed, "those who will not take seriously the authority and transformative power of the Pentateuch and the rest of the First Testament have no right to appeal, nor grounds for appealing, to the book of Psalms in worship" (p. 6). In order to be faithful to God in Christ, the whole testimony of Scripture must come to bear on the life of the believer and in the practice of the church.

In biblical theology, moving from the OT to the NT is often difficult given the continuities and discontinuities between the testaments. Yet at the end of each chapter, Block shows that what we know of worship in the NT has been established first in the OT, in most cases with greater detail and instruction. Thus, Block accomplishes theological moves with characteristic alacrity, sensitivity, and a view toward the benefit of the church.

And yet I take issue with Block's major statement that "unless the NT expressly declares the First Testament notions [of worship] obsolete, they continue" (pp. 7, 25). This view is prevalent throughout the book with obvious implications for tricky subjects like sabbatarianism. Overall, Block leans too heavily on the OT to the neglect of the NT. From Block's perspective, the OT is the "gift" of Christian worship while the NT simply makes a "contribution." This drives a hard wedge between the testaments on the topic of worship, much like dispensationalism. The NT is an afterthought in each chapter, comprising the final page or few paragraphs. This practice wrongly dichotomizes the OT from the NT. If one is to be biblical, then there is no avoiding that Jesus and the apostles encourage the church to read the OT anew with a view toward Christ. Thus, we can no longer treat OT texts without that view, because in light of Christ the OT books are now Christian books. They concern Jesus (Luke 24:27) and are about Jesus (24:44). Paul, at the end of his life, likewise reads and teaches the Bible with a view toward Jesus. He spends his last days "testifying to the kingdom of God and trying to convince them about Jesus both from the *Law of Moses and from the Prophets*" (Acts 28:23, 31; emphasis added).

The overemphasis on the OT in worship has implications in other areas as well, and Block is not always consistent. For example, in the chapter on sacrifices and offerings of worship, Block goes out of his way to show that there is no trace of messianic anticipation in the Pentateuch, and that the substitutionary nature of a once-for-all sacrifice is out of place (p. 255). Yet a few pages over (pp. 257ff.), in discussing the pattern of the tabernacle that Moses perceived in Exodus 25 and 40, Block states to the contrary that "Moses apparently saw the true heavenly dwelling of YHWH and then received instructions to have the Israelites construct a replica in which the sacrifices and rituals would represent *the singular heavenly sacrifice of the true Lamb of God*" (p. 258, emphasis added). Further down the same page, Blocks writes, "the replica tabernacle and its rituals pointed to YHWH's heavenly temple and *the sacrifice of Jesus Christ* to which the triune God had committed himself before the foundation of the world" (emphasis added). This seems to me to be a description of a substitutionary sacrifice, the type of which the apostles in the NT pointed so frequently to convince first-century Jews that they had been reading the OT wrong all along. "The gospel was preached to Abraham beforehand," Paul says (Gal 3:8). Jesus himself, "beginning with Moses" (Luke 24:27), interprets for his disciples the things "concerning himself." In this way, the OT sacrificial system does point to Jesus, the Lamb of God.

A final area of disagreement is with Block's contention that verbal expressions of one's own love for God have no biblical warrant: "No one in the First Testament ever tells God, 'I love you.' Appeals to love God are common (Deut 6:5), but no authors or characters have the audacity to claim that they measure up to the standard demanded by the word" (p. 238). After reading this statement one may think of Psalm 18:1, which is customarily translated, "I love you, O LORD." Block's footnote (p. 238 n. 54) does not clarify the matter. Block contends that the object of רחם is missing in Psalm 18:1 because it would be presumptuous to declare explicitly his love for God. Thus, Block says we should not sing songs that are self-laudatory, songs about our love for God instead of his love for us (p. 238). But this view overstates the point. Appeals to love God in the Bible are not simply common, but ubiquitous. What about the greatest commandment? If one has a correct theology of love coupled with a correct theology of worship as Block has outlined, is it not good and appropriate for that person to express love for God in their worship?

This point about love language for God leads to an issue I frequently see in worship books/conferences/websites, and *For the Glory of God* is no exception. On the issue of criticizing worship songs, there is no end. What authors typically do is cite bad worship songs and then lump all non-hymns into that category. The songs that Block criticizes in *For the Glory of God*, for example, are so old as to be irrelevant

("Father, I Adore You" [p. 51], "I Love You Lord" [p. 238], "Come As You Are" [p. 56]). There are perhaps some churches that still utilize those three songs, but these songs are not the norm. It is true that these songs place an inordinate amount of emphasis on one's personal relationship to God rather than his work in believers, but this does not mean that contemporary worship songs are bereft of theological content. There is a bevy of good songwriters producing theologically rich music/songs for the church today, writers like Bob Kauflin, Stuart Townend, Keith Getty, Aaron Keyes, Matt Papa, Shane Bernard, Ross King, Aaron Ivey, Brooks Ritter, Sandra McCracken, Mike Cosper, Matt Boswell, and more. Perhaps Block is not aware of these songwriters, but the accessibility that music leaders have to good church music today is astounding. Thus, I agree with Block that pastors should be sensitive and careful about song selections. If pastors are choosing poor worship songs or hymns for their services, then they are starving their congregations, who will eventually find themselves theologically malnourished. Finding good content is not the problem since that content is easily accessible. But I do not agree that the songs Block chose to criticize represent the whole.

These criticisms aside, to say that Block has written *the book* on the theology of worship is an understatement. I know of no other work that is as comprehensive as this one for the topic. Peterson, Due, Ross and others have all made significant contributions, to be sure, and yet the impressive scope and exegesis of Block's work stands apart. Young scholars should take note: doing a *biblical theology* begins not with themes, concepts, and ideas, but with the actual words of the Bible. And to that topic, Block is unrivaled. He is biblically faithful. We should also take note that Block's exegesis and application come from decades of teaching and writing about this topic. Let us not be quick to publish our views without seriously pondering the text over a long period of time. Block is a model on this point, and we should be grateful.

And yet if read with a closed mind and without pastoral sensitivity, this work could also serve as the church curmudgeon's handbook. The testimony of church history attests to the wide variety of opinions and practices for worship, and now *For the Glory of God* offers yet another. Even so, I have benefited from this book, and, if anything, Block has caused me to "look to the book," as it were, and like the Bereans in Acts 17, to go back to the Bible and test all things against the testimony of Scripture as I plan worship services.

Joshua M. Philpot
Founders Baptist Church

The Artistic Dimension: Literary Explorations of the Hebrew Bible by Keith Bodner. LHBOTS 590. London/New York: Bloomsbury T&T Clark, 2013. x + 209 pp., US $29.95, softcover.

In this volume, Keith Bodner provides a collection of ten engaging essays devoted to various kinds of literary analysis of biblical texts. Bodner, a professor at Crandall University, is certainly qualified to engage in this type of interdisciplinary work, as he possesses the rare advantage of holding earned doctorates in both English Literature and Biblical Studies. While half the chapters (comprising the first two sections) of this book have been previously published as journal articles, the overall coherence and value of this collection as a whole more than justifies their reproduction here.

Bodner's introduction helpfully situates his work in the context of the widespread disenchantment with traditional source criticism and related approaches due to their inability to illuminate the text for the average reader. After contextualizing his interests in the milieu of continuing the project pioneered by (but not only by) Robert Alter and Michael Fishbane, he gives a short summary of each essay.

The first part of the book is entitled, "Textual Problems and Literary Analysis," and it engages with the often-neglected stylistic implications of textual variants and contrasting tendencies throughout different manuscript traditions. The opening essay, "Crime Scene Investigation: A Text-Critical Mystery and the Strange Death of Ishbosheth," takes as its point of departure the considerable discrepancies between the MT and LXX versions of 2 Sam 4:5–7. Most notably, the LXX adds a doorkeeper that Rechab and Baanah must evade, while the MT seems to have them entering the house and committing the murder twice. After surveying previous text-critical approaches to the passage, Bodner provides a close reading of the unique nuances of the two versions of the story. Most notable are his insights that only the MT details deceptive measures taken by the two brothers and only the MT has specific vocabulary linking this murder with another murder committed by a pair of brothers, the murder of Abner back in 2 Sam 3 (which has implications for David's rule).

The next essay, "The Locutions of 1 Kings 22:28: A New Proposal," suggests that the second statement in this verse "Listen all you people!" should be attributed to Ahab instead of Micaiah. This novel interpretation has several intriguing implications for the story: Ahab can be understood as mimicking and mocking prophetic speech, his immediate use of the disguise continues this theme of deception, and Ahab ironically dies in front of "many people" in the ensuing battle. This section concludes with a short piece, "The 'Embarrassing Syntax' of

Psalm 47:10: A (Pro)vocative Option," in which Bodner surveys the immense amount of trouble commentators have had in making sense of the verse. His solution is to render the phrase "people of the God of Abraham" as a vocative, an option which has the twin attractions of retaining the reading of the MT and making superb interpretive sense.

The second part of the book, "Readers of the Lost Ark," focuses on the Ark Narrative of 1 Sam 4–6. It begins with a review article, "Arkeology: Shifting Emphases in 'Ark Narrative' Scholarship." Here, Bodner summarizes twelve key analysis of the Ark Narrative published between 1984 and 2003. While it is unsurprising that synchronic concerns supplanted diachronic approaches over time, he also finds that new scholars pay greater attention to its meaning for an exilic audience. Additionally, a number of questions relating to literary foreshadowing and thematic structures are raised by Bodner as possibilities for future research.

In "Mouse Trap: A Text-Critical Problem with Rodents in the Ark Narrative," Bodner begins with the observation that while both the MT and LXX of 1 Sam 6:4 mentions tumors and mice being included in the guilt offering of the Philistines to the Israelites, only the LXX includes a reference to mice previously in the story, as mice, along with tumors, are part of God's judgment against the Ashdodites in 1 Sam 5:6. The implications of this variant for the two versions of this story are organized by the categories of plot, character, and point of view.

Part Three of *The Artistic Dimension* is simply entitled "Further Soundings." Its first essay, "Jonathan Son of Abiathar: The Fulfillment of a Prophetic Word About the Dissolution of a Priestly Line," isolates four appearances of Jonathan and their significance for the concept of succession. Bodner argues that the use of Jonathan (coming from a toppled line of power) to inform Adonijah of Solomon's enthronement in 1 Kgs 1:43–48 suggests to the reader that even Solomon's line is far from secure.

Bodner switches to wisdom literature with "Highway to Sheol: Seductive Speech and Wisdom Literature in Proverbs 7." He walks through the chapter, paying special attention to the descriptions of the characters and particularly the slippery rhetoric of the unfaithful wife. For example in Prov 7:14–17, the mention of offerings and vows not only suggest piety on the part of the woman, but indicate a sumptuous meal may be available. Additionally, the spices used to perfume her bed are also what one would use to prepare a dead body, creating a hint of death in the discourse.

In Part Four, Bodner takes the reader into "The World of Chronicles." Its opening essay, "The Royal Skull in a Temple of Doom: An Interpretation of 1 Chronicles 10:10," centers around the diverging fates of Saul's dead body in 1 Sam 31:10 and 1 Chron 10:10, which differ in both specific body parts mentioned and location. Bodner argues that in Chronicles, the relocation of Saul's corpse to the temple of Dagon is an appropriate end for a king who failed to inquire of the Lord (1 Chr 10:14). It also provides a powerful contrast to the centrality of the Jerusalem temple which dominates the focus of much of the Chronicler's history.

In "Abijah's Elevated Rhetoric and the Civil War of 2 Chronicles 13," Bodner gives a helpful analysis of the various tactics used by Abijah to characterize, and project certain social roles for himself and Jeroboam. Finally, in "Capital Punishment: The Configuration of Ahaziah's Last Hours in 2 Chronicles 22," Bodner looks at the contrasting circumstances of the death of Ahaziah in 2 Chr 22 (hiding in Samaria) versus 2 Kgs 9 (fleeing to Megiddo). In his analysis, the version found in Chronicles can be explained by noting the symbolic relationship with compromise often connected with Samaria in Chronicles. This is followed by a brief conclusion chapter that reflects on the importance of dialogue through many of the essays and sketches out some possibilities of this kind of analysis for the book of Jeremiah.

This volume contains a number of innovative and exciting readings of biblical texts, and would contain much to interest any student, pastor, or scholar. While most of the chapters are written accessibly, at times Bodner provides summaries of previous approaches to a topic that differ enough from his research questions that may confuse nonspecialist readers. Some of this material may have been best placed in the footnotes. Additionally, a couple of the essays contain considerable excursuses that tread far beyond the main subject matter of the essay in question. This may be surprising to readers looking to quickly discover his conclusion or central points, and some use of organizational devices would have been helpful in these cases. However, neither of these factors detract from the quality and excellence of this volume.

DAVID J. FULLER
McMaster Divinity College

Evil Within and Without: The Source of Sin and Its Nature as Portrayed in Second Temple Literature by Myryam T. Brand. JAJS 9. Göttingen: Vandenhoeck & Ruprecht, 2013. 331 pp., €89.99, hardcover.

This careful and comprehensive study, the published version of the author's doctoral thesis, explores the concept of sin in Second Temple Jewish texts. The key question is, as the title suggests, whether sin is an act which stems from a person's own self (i.e., sin being a part of the human make-up) or whether it comes from the outside and influences receptive persons. Brand's study builds on a staggering amount of already existing secondary literature. Brand does not aim to offer new interpretations of individual texts but instead to highlight the wide *variety* of approaches to sin in the Second Temple literature. Her study challenges the common scholarly tendency to expect theological consistency with regard to the origin of sin; her own broad analysis of the material demonstrates how anachronistic such a view is. Furthermore, it emphasizes the importance of not "reading into" one text the views of another text. In addition, her analysis explores (1) the role that views pertaining to the origin of sin play in determining who is part of a given community, and (2) the notions of determinism versus free will, i.e., whether people can choose to do God's will or whether their righteousness is predetermined by God.

The study progresses systematically through an impressively wide range of material. The material is organized along an envisioned line, beginning at one end with those texts which depict the source of evil as internal ("human inclination to sin"), and concluding at the other end with those texts which understand evil as due to external sources ("demonic influence"). This line is meant to be neither chronological nor geographical: there are contemporaneous texts from the same geographical location which display different and sometimes also mutually conflicting views. All the discussed texts are Jewish in origin, composed between 400 B.C.E. to 100 C.E. Ideally, this set of texts should also have included much of the New Testament, yet given the uniqueness of this material, Brand ultimately decides to exclude it (p. 28). This exclusion does not mean New Testament texts are not being considered, however. Brand makes several pertinent comparisons between the material under investigation and especially Pauline thought, something which renders this book useful also to New Testament scholars.

In her study, Brand covers the following material: sectarian and non-sectarian material from Qumran, *Ben Sira*, the writings of Philo of Alexandria, *4 Ezra, 2 Baruch, 1 Enoch*, and *Jubilees*. Over the course of 11 chapters, she explores how select material from each text portrays sin. In a few cases, the same text appears in more than one chapter. For instance, different parts of the *Community Rule* feature different ideas vis-à-vis the origin of sin. In her investigation, Brand highlights the significance of genre. The prayer genre tends to emphasize the gap between God and the supplicant, the innate inclination to sin, the inability of the sinner to amend her ways, and the urgent need for divine assistance. In contrast, covenantal texts combine the notions of an inherent human inclination toward sin with the human ability to fight the same inclination. The fact that humans are prone to sin cannot be an excuse for sinning. Rather, every person has the free will to choose righteousness. Turning to the wisdom texts of Ben Sira and the writings of Philo, yet another aspect comes to the forefront, namely the desire to distance human sin from God and to clarify that each person is responsible for their own actions, be they evil or good. Finally, in texts written after the destruction of Jerusalem in 70 C.E., *4 Ezra* in particular testifies to a more pessimistic view of human free will: unless God assists the struggling human being, that person has little chance of resisting her innate inclination to sin. Alone, the temptation to succumb to sin is near irresistible, an insight which, in turn, challenges the notion of free will. Moreover, *4 Ezra* debates and ultimately rejects the widespread notion that the law can assist a person in her struggle to triumph over her sinful tendency (cf. Rom 7:7–13).

Turning to the second half of the book, devoted to texts which stress the connection between sin and demonic influence, Brand explores the origin of evil as attested by the Watcher tradition preserved in *1 Enoch* 15 and argues that this tradition is used to explain the origin of *natural evil* rather than the origin of sin. For the latter, we have to wait until *Jubilees*, which employs the same myth to explicate how demons came into the world and how they are a source of evil influence. Humans can, however, fight off their influence through prayer and by keeping the law. Humans still have free will to act righteously, despite the belief that their innate evil inclination is caused by demonic powers. Yet other texts reflect the belief that some people are ruled by demonic powers and thus destined to commit sins, while other people receive divine support which enables them to keep to the path of justice.

In many of these texts, the underlying issue is one of community identity. Gentiles in general are characterized by their evil inclination/demonic emissaries and it is thus entirely natural for them to sin and thus to persecute Israel. Along the same lines of thinking, some of the Qumran texts differentiate between, on the one hand, non-members who are ruled by their evil leaders who, in turn, are ruled by Belial and his spirits and, on the other hand, members who are characterized by their ability to choose righteousness. In some cases, the very fact that a person is able to act righteously is a sign that a person is elected by God. Naturally, the performance of key righteous acts (such as keeping the correct calendar) may be the very matter that distinguishes members from non-members.

In sum, this is a very well researched and helpful book which demonstrates the wide range of attitudes towards the origin of sin in Second Temple Jewish literature. In addition, I hope that scholars dealing with these issues in the New Testament will benefit from this extensive and careful analysis of contemporary texts.

LENA-SOFIA TIEMEYER
University of Aberdeen

Psalms in Their Context: An Interpretation of Psalms 107–118 by John C. Crutchfield. Milton Keynes, England: Paternoster, 2009. xviii + 166 pp., US $22.00, softcover.

John Crutchfield is currently the Middle Eastern studies Program Director and an Associate Professor of Biblical Studies at Columbia International University. He studied under Alan Cooper, a student of Brevard Childs, at Union Theological Seminary. Thus, it is not surprising that his book adopts a canonical approach in the analysis of Pss 107–118.

The book consists of five chapters. This first includes a brief but accurate survey of Psalms scholarship that has adopted the canonical approach. Methodologically, Crutchfield also adopts the canonical approach but asks contextual questions at three widening compositional levels: (a) the immediate surrounding psalms; (b) the entire Psalter and; (c) the entire OT Canon (pp. 12–13). Chapters 2–4 neatly follow these three levels of analyses, and the final chapter concludes his analysis.

In chapter 2 Crutchfield studies every psalm of interest under the categories of genre, structure, compositional theories, and settings/intention. The "special features" and contextual issues of a given psalm are also analysed. An important conclusion reached in this chapter is Crutchfield's identification of the victimised speaker in Ps 109 and the "God-fearer" in Ps 112 as the "Davidic messiah" of Ps 110 (pp. 28–35). As such, he views the entirety of Pss 109–112 as messianic. Furthermore, Crutchfield argues that the "celebrant" in Ps 118 is "likened to Moses" and when seen together with Pss 109–112, "[the] only person who could be referred to with such language in this context is the expected messiah" (p. 54).

In chapter 3 Crutchfield extends his analysis of Pss 107–118 to the context of the entire Psalter. He starts by reviewing several redaction agendas of the Psalter as proposed by Brennan, Childs, Wilson, Walton, Brueggemann, Creach, Sheppard, and Mitchell. The conclusion that Crutchfield has reached after the review is careful and honest. He notes, "[at] this point, we could conclude that a redactional agenda with sufficient explanatory force has not yet been found; we could also conclude that a redactional agenda, though possible, is simply not discernable" (p. 80).

Instead of a single, all-encompassing agenda, Crutchfield argues for an identification of dominant themes in the books of the Psalter and their development across the Psalter (p. 80). He identifies three dominant trajectories at work in the Psalter: (a) sapiential; (b) eschatological; and (c) primacy of worship (p. 82). Crutchfield then analyzes how these trajectories are at work in Pss 107–118. For example, he sees a merging of the messianic-eschatological motifs in Pss 109–110 and the sapiential references in Pss 111–112. Psalms 113–117 trace God's work in Israel's history, culminating in a call for all nations to praise God's faithfulness. Furthermore, Ps 118 develops an understanding of a messiah already found elsewhere in the psalms. The messiah suffers (Pss 18, 22) and is pious (Pss 18, 45, 72, 89) yet will also be vindicated and exalted (p. 96).

In chapter 4 Crutchfield expands his analysis to the context of the entire OT. Three important connections highlighted include Hannah's prayer in 1 Sam 2, the Golden calf idolatry in Exod 32–34, and the Song of Moses in Exod 15. Crutchfield argues that these connections support the messianic interpretation of Pss 108–112, YHWH's faithfulness and the universal praise of those who call on him in Pss 107, 113–117, and identifying the Davidic king in Ps 118 as the "New Moses" (p. 129).

The final chapter summarizes Crutchfield's thesis and offers several avenues for further research. A discussion on the Dead Sea Scrolls is given in the appendix in which Crutchfield discusses how the Qumran Psalms are possibly redacted utilizing thematic and lexical connections.

Crutchfield's work is helpful in several aspects. It is clearly structured and written. His arguments are well presented and easy to follow. Each psalm in the group is also well analyzed. His survey of various proposals of the redaction agenda of the Psalter is sharp and accurate. His work has widened the scope of intertextual analysis of the Psalms and uncovered important intertextual connections. One of the unique contributions Crutchfield has brought to the canonical study of Pss 107–118 is the identification of the Davidic messiah in this group of psalms.

Three other points are also noteworthy. First, Crutchfield's methodology is primarily an intertextual analysis of semantic connections in widening contexts. Although Crutchfield situated his methodology under the canonical approach, we must note that intertextual analysis is not equivalent to canonical analysis of the psalms. Discussions on how superscriptions, poetic devices, and other structural techniques function canonically are only treated lightly. The question is whether the method of lexical/semantic inter-connection analyses can be the *primary* tool to uncover the redactional agenda (if there is one) in a poetic book such as the Psalter.

Second, an important lacuna in Crutchfield's widening circle of contextual analysis is how Pss 107–118 function *within Book V of the Psalter*. Crutchfield moves directly from the immediate context of these twelve psalms to the entire Psalter. If the widening contexts are important in the process of interpretation, it will be pertinent to understand how Pss 107–118 are first understood in Book V before their place in the entire Psalter.

Finally, we must note that Crutchfield's proposition of the three trajectories (sapiential, eschatological, praise) as the redactional agenda of the entire Psalter is *not* the result of his method of widening textual analyses or the development of his arguments. These proposed trajectories, identified over three pages of discussion (pp. 81–83), come *before* his analyses on Pss 107–118 within the context of the entire Psalter.

Nonetheless, Crutchfield's work is yet another important contribution to recent Psalms scholarship especially for the study of Book V of the Psalms. The messianic interpretations reached by him are certainly helpful in furthering the study of the Davidic king in the Psalter.

PETER C. W. HO
University of Gloucestershire

YHWH is King: The Development of Divine Kingship in Ancient Israel by Shawn W. Flynn. Leiden: Brill, 2014. xiii + 207 pp., US $133.00, hardcover.

Shawn W. Flynn is Assistant Professor of Religion and Theology at Saint Mark's College in Vancouver, Canada. *YHWH is King* is a revision of his Ph.D. dissertation undertaken at the University of Toronto. Flynn's study analyzes, as the subtitle implies, the development of YHWH's kingship in ancient Israel. Flynn notes that his work seeks to accomplish three things: 1) to classify the stages of YHWH's kingship; 2) to identify how YHWH's kingship is presented in each stage; and 3) to determine the motivation and context for the differences (p. 1).

Flynn begins by laying out the thesis that there is a discernable difference in the presentation of YHWH's kingship between Pss 93 and 95–99 and the presentation of his kingship in earlier texts (he particularly notes Exod 15; Num 23; Deut 33:5; and Ps 29). This difference can then be "informed by the developments of Marduk's kingship in Babylon as suitable parallels" (p. 1). YHWH's kingship is then presented as Judah's response to Neo-Assyrian imperialism. After laying out his thesis, Flynn surveys the literature on the topic, noting those who viewed YHWH's kingship in a static (as opposed to his dynamic) manner. He then moves to a discussion of methodologies for uncovering the development in YHWH's kingship. He is particularly focused on dating the texts in question through linguistic dating and by how divinity is portrayed in them. He ends the introduction with a discussion in the differences of the language use between early and late texts that concern YHWH's kingship.

Chapter 2 focuses on comparing the main texts in question. According to Flynn, the Psalms of YHWH's kingship (93, 95–99), which are deemed to be later texts, are concerned with showing God's universal reign as creator. The earlier texts (Exod 15; Num 23; and Ps 29), however, that are concerned with YHWH's kingship portray him as a divine warrior. The way in which YHWH's kingship is developed changes the form in which it is discussed. Psalm 29:1, for instance, mentions the heavenly counsel whereas Psalm 96:4–5 mentions that the gods are simply worthless idols. According to Flynn, because YHWH is the universal creator God of creation there is an emphasis away from the language of the divine counsel (pp. 40–41).

In the third chapter Flynn advances that the way to understand what is happening with the development in YHWH's kingship is to compare it to similar changes that occur elsewhere within the ANE. Flynn focuses on cultural translation, which is a methodology taken from social anthropology and informed by linguistic theory (p. 73). This chapter briefly discusses the use of cultural translation within Israelite religion. Flynn then discusses the previous limitations of this methodology and how it is used within its discipline to show how it can be further used within the study of Israelite religion. In doing this Flynn recognizes four areas that aid in identifying cultural translation between Israel and the ANE (pp. 87–89).

The fourth chapter goes on to discuss the four areas of cultural translation of Marduk's kingship, particularly within the *Enūma eliš* and its broader Mesopotamian context. Flynn's proposal is not that YHWH's kingship was necessarily patterned off a specific source, but that there was a cultural situation where the Israelites were exposed to the representation of Marduk as a universal creator with a warrior past. Flynn then advances that there was an elevation of Marduk to a universal creator within the *Enūma eliš* as a response to early Assyrian imperialism. This change in Marduk's kingship then "becomes an instructive historical analogue to understand YHWH's rise and kingship in Israel" (p. 118).

The fifth chapter delves into the context and motivations for YHWH's new kingship. Here Flynn advances that YHWH's kingship as presented in later texts is similar to Marduk's kingship in the *Enūma eliš*. This change in YHWH's kingship was precipitated by Neo-Assyrian imperialism. This new kingship of YHWH as a universal creator does not present him as competing with another deity because within the warrior deity model YHWH could not compete because of the superior strength of the Neo-Assyrian empire.

Flynn ends his study with a sixth chapter where he provides a brief summary of the points of his argument.

There are several admirable features of this work. First, Flynn shows a helpful integration of other disciplines within the study of the Old Testament. Flynn's use of anthropological, even cultural translation, is not new. Flynn does, however, more thoroughly use this methodology and explain its salient features. This study provides several thought-provoking and helpful insights into how the ANE can translate into a better understanding of practices within ancient Israel. This book will certainly further the conversation on the relevance of both anthropological methodologies in general, and cultural translation in particular, for biblical study.

Another helpful aspect of this study is that Flynn draws out two of the different aspects of YHWH's kingship within ancient Israelite thought. Despite whether one agrees with Flynn's diachronic reconstructions of the biblical text, his study does help to show that YHWH is presented within the Bible both as a divine warrior and as the universal creator.

Flynn's study contains helpful and meaningful content, but it will be helpful for the reader to know some of Flynn's presuppositions. First, his dating of texts is based upon a history of religions approach by which not all will be convinced. Flynn readily admits that he accepts that Israel's understanding of God moved from polytheism to monotheism (p. 16), and his study focuses on the diachronic development of YHWH's kingship from a divine warrior to a universal creator. Second, he seems too easily to dismiss divine warrior language in Ps 98:1–3. He notes that a warrior tradition is present (p. 4), but then states that the language in favor of the divine warrior theme "is almost absent" (p. 45). While the divine warrior theme may not be as thoroughly developed in Ps 98 as in Exod 15, a lack of large-scale development of this theme does not necessarily indicate that the idea had changed; perhaps the author is just wishing to communicate other facets of YHWH's kingship.

YHWH is King serves as a valuable addition to research on the kingship of God. It serves as a great complement to other major studies within this areas including the more recent works of Brettler (*God is King: Understanding an Israelite Metaphor*, Sheffield, 1989) and Moore (*Moving Beyond Symbol and Myth: Understanding the Kingship of God of the Hebrew Bible Through Metaphor*, Peter Lang, 2009). *YHWH is King* would be a beneficial resource for the advanced student or scholar interested in the subject of the kingship of God or the divine warrior motif.

DANIEL S. DIFFEY
Grand Canyon University

Huldah: The Prophet who Wrote Hebrew Scripture by Preston Kavanagh. Cambridge: Lutterworth, 2012. 220 pp., £17.00, softcover.

Preston Kavanagh's book provides a creative and expansive look at the figure of the prophet Huldah mentioned in 2 Kgs 22:14–20 and 2 Chr 34:22–28. Huldah sits among Miriam and Deborah as a womn in the Old Testament who held a prophetic role, was acknowledged for this role, and impacted Israelite history. Notably, Huldah's role in the time of Josiah includes her participation in a key revival as she validates a scroll called the "book of the Law," which was found during temple repairs that took place under King Josiah's reign.

Unlike Jeremiah, Ezekiel, and Zephaniah, Huldah's contemporaries who are well known due to their status as authors of Old Testament books, Huldah's role as prophetess is less frequently noted and, unfortunately, her role is often overlooked despite her actual importance in history. Recently Huldah has received revived interest, particularly among feminist interpreters whose goal is to bring to the fore otherwise overlooked women in Scripture.

Kavanagh locates his book in this vein of research, pointing to the under appreciation of Huldah despite being, as he suggests, "among the most influential women in human history" (p. 1). Toward this end, Kavanagh uses a wide range of methods to demonstrate Huldah's importance. As Kavanagh has done in his previous books, *Secrets of the Jewish Exile* (2005), *The Exilic Code* (2009), and *The Shaphan Group* (2011), Kavanagh looks for the secret codes in Scripture based on a combination of complex methods including "athbash, anagrams, probabilities, and encoded spellings." In this book, Kavanagh argues "that Huldah first became the wife of Judah's King Jehoiakim and the queen mother to Jehoiachin, her son, who succeeded his father, Jehoiakim, on the throne" (p. 1). Moreover, using these methods Kavanagh argues that Huldah was also an "elder, author, advisor, merchant, prophet, priestess, and commanding general," and subsequently she became "head of the Asherah cult" (p. 1).

Kavanagh argues for this biographical history of Huldah in chapters 2–4 after introducing his methodology in chapter 1. In chapter

5, Kavanagh argues that invectives against Huldah by Huldah's critics can be found in nearly all of Scripture, ranging from Pentateuch to the prophets via codes. In chapters 6–10, Kavanagh uses his approach to argue that Huldah had a hand in writing or was the subject of most of the Hebrew Scriptures. According to Kavanagh, Huldah wrote with Daniel and Ezra portions of their work (Kavanagh also dates Ezra to the exilic period; p. 79). Kavanagh suggests that Huldah held a key role among the Deuteronomists in writing the Deuteronomic History and that Huldah created characters like Deborah (p. 82) and Abigail (p. 84) (ch. 7); Huldah edited substantial portions of Genesis and Exodus (ch. 8); Proverbs represents the assault upon and defense of Huldah (ch. 9). According to chapter 10, Huldah is linked to the composition of 18 psalms—some were against her (Ps 116), about her (Ps 143), and the rest of the 16 were by her.

While one appreciates the need for scholarship on pivotal women in the Old Testament, Kavanagh's book inflates scant evidence via a series of complex mathematics based on very specific theories developed around codes in Scripture, and Kavanagh's work suffers from an over dependence on his own prior research. While it is common for scholars to build on their previous arguments, Kavanagh's book is marked by a lack of scholarly engagement with secondary sources who hold different perspectives than him on a wide variety of topics such as dating, the roles of figures in Old Testament history, etc. A glance at Kavanagh's footnotes reveals his lack of engagement with other scholars compared to the extensive use of his own work, referenced on roughly a third of the book's pages. This tends to create a false picture within Kavanagh's work of greater evidence than actually exists to establish and support his overall thesis. Consequently, he creates a book that lacks the scholarly depth and breadth necessary to engage the broader scholarly guild.

One can also question the validity of Kavanagh's methods. For example, Kavanagh's "coded spellings" approach states that the use of only one Hebrew character from consecutive text words can spell a name (p. 5). With the name "Huldah," this means that every use of the Hebrew letters *he, lamed,* and *dagesh* in any configuration can be a reference to Huldah's name. This allows Kavanagh to argue that Huldah's name is everywhere, when it may simply be the case that *these letters* are everywhere. Kavanagh acknowledges that biblical scholars have questioned his reliance on codings in the Masoretic Text for two reasons: 1) the long history of scribal emendations make coding unlikely, and 2) the MT is one of several surviving texts of the Old Testament and therefore not wholly the original text. While Kavanagh tries to argue against these criticisms (pp. 5–6), these critiques still stand as major barriers for Kavanagh's method.

Part of the overall problem with Kavanagh's work is his intention to connect almost every female figure or reference to female equality to Huldah. For example, he points to Huldah as the one "who penned . . . 'Let us make humankind in our image,'" claims that she is both Lady Wisdom and the Good Wife in the book of Proverbs, and that "what appear to be her own writings about Deborah, Abigail, Bathsheba, Tamar, and Rebecca almost certainly conceal autobiographical elements" (p. 2). Yet at the same time, Kavanagh aligns Huldah with Asherah worship in her later life to explain the loss of her credibility among the prophets. He argues that Huldah is secretly named via code as the Levite's wife who is raped and dismembered in Judg 9 (p. 2) and is similarly pointed to as the intended victim in the case of Jephthah's daughter (p. 62), showing the viciousness of Huldah's critics. Thus, what seems to be a tale that heralds a positive story for womenkind instead ultimately ends in male violence according to Kavanagh's arguments. However, Kavanagh's comments about Huldah's fault are telling of an underlying problem in Kavanagh's approach: Huldah is discredited ultimately because she is a woman. As Kavanagh explains, "Given the tenor of her criticism, one must conclude that another of Huldah's faults was that her gender was female" (p. 2).

Kavanagh's purpose appears to be in line with a broader feminist agenda of unearthing and praising female figures in Scripture. He explicitly mentions feminist scholars like Elisabeth Schüssler Fiorenza (pp. 8–9), Phyllis Bird (pp. 8–9), Sarah Pomeroy (indirectly via Judith Wegner) (p. 9), and Phyllis Trible (p. 62). However, several aspects of his approach actually move in the opposite direction. First, in order to praise Huldah as comprehensively included in Scripture, Kavanagh must suggest that other stories of women in Scripture are *less* about *their own* stories and *more* about *Huldah*. In a sense, this is robbing from Paul to pay Peter. If Deborah's or Abigail's or Tamar's stories are *really* stories about Huldah, we have lost the story of several women to one woman (according to Kavanagh, "Abigail is Huldah . . . It appears that Huldah created Abigail, fashioning her in the prophet's own image" [p. 84]). This is not a triumph for feminism but a great loss. Kavanagh has set up a situation in which one woman's voice becomes the dominant voice at the expense of her fellow women's voices. Similarly, attributing Lady Wisdom to Huldah creates a situation in which personification of God as Lady Wisdom loses its depth and richness. This has potential implications not only for feminist approaches to Old Testament theology but also for New Testament theology.

Another problem with Kavanagh's approach in relation to the potential value of this book for raising the profile of women is that Kavanagh almost completely ignores many of the major women scholars who have been writing on Huldah over the years. In fact, nearly all of Kavanagh's interaction with female scholars happens in only two sections totaling four pages of the entire 200-page book (pp. 8–10, 62). With the exception of one reference to Wilda Gafney's work on women prophets (p. 32), Kavanagh appears unaware of the major work that has been done by women scholars on Huldah, including the work of Renita Weems ("Huldah, the Prophet: Reading a [Deuteronomistic] Woman's Identity"), Diana Edelman ("Huldah the Prophet—of Yahweh or Asherah?"), Claudia Camp ("Huldah"), and Esther Fuchs (, "Prophecy and the Construction of Women: Inscriptive and Erasure"). In fact, scholars like Edelman could have helped Kavanagh to shape his argument along more scholarly lines as Edelman's 1994 theory proves strikingly similar to Kavanagh's theories regarding Huldah as priestess of Asherah. Kavanagh neglects to mention this similarity.

Kavanagh's entire project claims to value a woman's voice (Huldah) that has been unappreciated, yet his entire method undervalues the women's voices in biblical scholarship that have been working to raise Huldah's profile. In fact, overlooking these female scholars (as well as male scholars on Huldah [notably, Pieter Willem van der Horst, "Huldah's Tomb in Early Jewish Tradition"]), Kavanagh suggests that his book "seeks to measure—for the first time ever—the extraordinary impact of Huldah the prophetess upon Hebrew Scriptures" (p. 1). Yet, Kavanagh cannot claim that this is the "first time ever" that Huldah's impact has been appreciated when stacks of scholarly articles and chapters in books by articulate female scholars (and male scholars) would prove otherwise.

Thus, while Kavanagh's book promises to shed light on a much-neglected female figure in Scripture—and this is a noble goal—Kavanagh's approach actually hides the voices of women who have sought to make Huldah's voice heard and does not provide a convincing case for his particular picture of this woman Huldah despite her value for history and Scripture.

BETH STOVELL
Ambrose University

Ancient Israel's History. An Introduction to Issues and Sources edited by Bill T. Arnold and Richard S. Hess. Grand Rapids, MI: Baker Academic, 2014, xv + 544 pp., US $44.99, hardcover.

The study of the history of ancient Israel is important for theology. It illuminates considerable parts of Scripture and shows that the Christian faith is closely related to the history of mankind and to ordinary life. It reveals that a scholarly approach to these areas is a matter of craftsmanship and method, but also of worldview and theology. Moreover, the discipline touches upon the very nature of God himself, who reveals himself in history, and highlights that even in Old Testament times, only a minority of the people living in Israel and Judah shared the views of the writings that later became the canonical books.

Before World War II, the topic was only an aspect in studying the content of the biblical books and in describing the history of ancient Israelite religion. Since, however, the "history of (ancient) Israel" has become a separate course in the theological curriculum. First, the classic overviews by Martin Noth and John Bright served as a help. Over the last decade and a half, new textbooks have appeared, mostly dominated by the methodological problems of the fierce minimalist-maximalist debate. This focus on method has been illuminating, as becomes evident from, for instance, the presentation of the biblical history of Israel by Iain Provan, V. Philips Long, and Tremper Longman III (Westminster John Knox, 2003), and in the survey of critical issues by Brad E. Kelle and Megan Bishop Moore (Eerdmans, 2011). At the same time, however, the minimalist-maximalist debate turned out to be a dead end. Caught in the (late-)modern dichotomy of absolute certainty and total chaos and a blind spot for the practical limitations of scholarly inquiry or theological reasoning, the permanent assessment of the question for the historicity of the events as described in the Bible led to historical discussions in which it became very hard to do justice to the diversity of the biblical texts and to the nature of non-biblical textual and material remains.

Accordingly, it is praiseworthy that Bill T. Arnold (Asbury Theological Seminary) and Richard S. Hess (Denver Seminary) undertook the effort to look beyond the struggles of the past decades by creating a multi-authored volume in which specialists introduce both students and scholars to the basic sources and issues of the most important periods in ancient Israel's history. The book presents a variety of views and methodological approaches. What holds them in common, Hess writes in his introduction, is "a respect for the biblical text as a legitimate source in the study of Israel's history" (p. 4). His introduction offers a concise history of the discipline and discusses some basic issues, such as chronology. Hess also observes three general directions in present research: scholars who read the sources suspiciously and build their history from social science models; a critical orthodoxy standing in the line of Noth; and histories trying to balance biblical and extra-biblical sources. Hess rightly admits that the last approach has its weaknesses. In his view, however, it is still best to examine the story as it is traditionally told and to study the major critical issues by trying to understand the sources (p. 19).

In some ways, this is a daring view. Unlike most recent reconstructions of the story of ancient Israel, the book does not start with the emergence of Israel (and Judah) in the southern Levant, but with three chapters on "Pentateuchal material" having a special historiographical interest. Arnold opens with a rich essay on the question of the nature of the Book of Genesis. What in this "mytho-historical narrative" (Gen 1–11), "traditional epic" (Gen 12–36) and "novel" (Gen 37–50) can be characterized as factual, likely, plausible, or possible? James Hoffmeier, Egyptologist and archaeologist, offers an excellent summary of his research in the Nile Delta and the Sinai as well as its implications for the Exodus and wilderness narratives while also maintaining that external support for these narratives is not a prerequisite for regarding them as authentic. Samuel Greengus in turn discusses the Pentateuchal covenants and treaties in their relation to the corpus of similar texts in the ancient Near East. His overview of contextual material leads to the conclusion that, for instance, the parallels between Deuteronomy and the Neo-Assyrian treaties can be explained by the fact that both contain traditional curse themes.

The rest of the chapters turn to history itself. Lawson G. Stone discusses the emergence of early Israel in Canaan by integrating as much information as possible and comes to the interesting, but also speculative, conclusion that Pharaoh Merenptah's campaign against Canaan was a reaction to the invasion of the Israelite tribes. Robert D. Miller II has accepted the challenge to incorporate historical information from the book of Judges in his anthropological perspective on the tribal nuclei in the Iron Age I highlands. Daniel Bodi again explores his hypothesis that the books of Samuel reflect West Semitic patterns in telling stories about the rise of tribal chieftains and kings. Steven M. Ortiz challenges the idea that there has been no United Monarchy by offering a synopsis of recent archaeological research into perspective. James K. Mead offers a thorough historical framework for his previous literary studies of stories about prophets in the book of Kings and discusses the parallels with the prophecies from Mari and at the Neo-Assyrian court.

Finally, entering more firm historical ground, Kyle Greenwood and Sandra Richter explore the late-tenth-, ninth- and eighth-century issues and Brad E. Kelle discusses the complex situation of Judah during the seventh century. In addition, Peter van der Veen shows his epigraphical and archaeological skills with regard to the period of destruction, exile, and return, while André Lemaire and David A. deSilva offer their reconstruction of the history of the southern Levant during the Persian and Hellenistic periods.

Despite the book being called an "introduction," the volume offers a huge amount of information, challenging students and scholars with new information or creative reorganizations of well-known material. Nevertheless, as a scholar from Europe, I was particularly interested that the major excavation by Kathleen Kenyon is not mentioned among the major excavations in Jerusalem. Further, important literature from Germany is missing, for instance by Manfred and Helga Weippert. I also desired more explicit interaction in the introduction with the methodological debates in the European Seminar of Historical Methodology as published in the volumes edited by Lester Grabbe (Sheffield Academic Press/T&T Clark, 1997–2015; for my own review of the project, see the *Festschrift* for Margreet Steiner, T&T Clark, 2014). Finally, it seems that the publications of Kenneth Kitchen and Paul Lawrence on treaties, law, and covenant in the ancient Near East (Harrassowitz, 2012) and of Avraham Faust on Judah in the Neo-Babylonian period (Society of Biblical Literature, 2012) were published too late to act as serious discussion partners for Greengus and Van der Veen (cf. p. 91, mentioning Kitchen and Lawrence).

As always, questions arise, too. For the sake brevity, I mention only a few hot topics. Several chapters refer to the "Deuteronomistic History" (e.g., pp. 286, 351, 370). But what does that mean? That the major part of Deuteronomy–2 Kings was written after 621 B.C.? Or was there—as I am personally inclined to believe—some kind of "deuteronomic" or "deuteronomistic" historiographical tradition, which began long before the cultic reforms by Hezekiah and Josiah? This is an issue that matters both historically and theologically. In addition, not all evangelical readers will embrace Arnold's moderate use of the Documentary Hypothesis and his characterizations of the book of Genesis. However, his instructive essay is an excellent starter for a discussion with students on the question of what a theologian can actually say about this book from a scholarly, historical perspective. They will at least learn that it is not easy to formulate an alternative. A third topic regards Bodi's use of texts from Mari and Alalakh in his effort to illuminate narrative patterns in the book of Samuel (pp. 204–23). In order to be successful, a comparison or analogy needs to be grounded in a historical process, offering plausible mechanisms for transmission and balancing generalities and particularities in the texts. Bodi did not entirely convince me in this respect. At the same time, it is laudable that he does have a clear view of the biblical text. In a historical debate, the general assumption regarding its trustworthiness is not enough, as this will be perceived as a protective strategy privileging biblical claims. Also, it too often results in political readings not taking into account the text's rhetoric and theological purposes. Accordingly, the few pages with Ortiz's general remarks on the biblical testimony regarding the United Monarchy could have easily been omitted from the book. In a similar way, I highly doubt his assumption that the list of Solomonic prefects in 1 Kgs 4:7–19 claims to offer a division of administrative districts (p. 249). In my view, both text and archaeology tend toward a different, much more moderate direction.

This brings me to the major problem, not only in this volume, but also in writing a history of ancient Israel in general. Biblical historiography is clearly to be defined as referential literature. But a real appreciation of its literary and theological aims also implies that the texts mostly offer a very incomplete picture of the actual social, economic, and political developments. They were not written as annalistic accounts, but to tell about God. Accordingly, we do not always know in what manner the texts refer to history. In addition, they give way to a whole range of historical reconstructions. The study of non-biblical texts and the application socio-archaeological models as heuristic devices in interpreting material remains should be used to fill in this gap. But how? It is the historian's primary impulse to arrange all the material in such a way that his own reconstruction appears to be most plausible. Most of the time this impulse prevails, despite the fact that both the biblical and non-biblical evidence leave room for much more scenarios. What then, is the best way to do justice to Scripture and to the scholarly enterprise itself?

Reading *Ancient Israel's History* again made me think that it would be better to take more time in sketching the range of diverse possibilities. At the same time, the overall picture of the volume with its clear and well-informed essays shows exactly what today's study of ancient Israel's history is about: a cacophony of competing narratives in a methodological minefield. Therefore, the authors should be thanked for their efforts. This is definitely a great textbook for any serious course in the history of ancient Israel.

KOERT VAN BEKKUM
Theological University Kampen, Netherlands

Bound for the Promised Land: The Land Promise in God's Redemptive Plan by Oren R. Martin. NSBT 34. Downers Grove, IL: IVP, 2015. 208 pp., US $25.00, softcover.

This volume by Oren R. Martin is a "substantial revision" (p. 11) of his Ph.D. dissertation, "Bound for the Kingdom: The Land Promise in God's Redemptive Plan" (2013). Martin completed his dissertation at The Southern Baptist Theological Seminary, and he now serves at Boyce College (Southern's undergraduate institution) as Assistant Professor of Christian Theology.

One immediately notices that Martin's program in *Bound for the Promised Land* is expansive: he traces the land promises from the opening chapters of Genesis to the final chapters of Revelation. Since treatments of this important motif are characteristically "embedded in works that cover much broader topics" (p. 18 n. 2), Martin aims at providing a "whole-Bible biblical theology" that focuses specifically on the titular topic (see esp. p. 19 n. 7). As for methodology, and to his credit, Martin shows awareness of his conservative presuppositions about the nature of the Bible (pp. 27–28) as he proceeds in light of Richard Lints's three horizons of redemptive interpretation: textual, epochal, and canonical (p. 25). The study takes the Old and New Testaments as "a unified text with a developing story" (p. 25). Thus *Bound for the Promised Land* proceeds to explain how God's land promises to Abraham addresses the loss of the kingdom in Eden while also serving as a "type" in Israel's history and scriptures. This type anticipates fulfillment in the New Testament's presentation of a greater land that results from the work and person of Jesus Christ and, ultimately, in a new heaven and new earth. The Abrahamic promises, then, play out in a "progressive fulfilment of God's kingdom on earth" across the entire biblical narrative.

With any project this expansive, it is reasonable to expect some gaps. The scope is simply too vast to cover every text or collection in the Bible. Martin's work is no exception; however, I found his selection of texts for the project on point and well thought out. Nothing under investigation is unnecessary. That said, I did find some omissions in the Old Testament treatments at least curious, if not problematic. At this point, it is necessary to point out that my own specialization is Old Testament; thus, I bring my own biases and preferences to this engagement of *Bound for the Promised Land*. Still, there are some noticeable omissions of texts, at least from my perspective.

Some of these texts concern the Pentateuch. Martin is right to devote an entire chapter to Genesis (i.e., ch. 3); and, his division of this chapter into Gen 1—11 and 12—50 makes sense. He deftly connects the loss of the kingdom in the former to the land promises and the patriarchs in the latter. The following chapter (ch. 4), however, only deals with Exodus and Deuteronomy. Although I think issues of holy worship and holy living in Leviticus might have an important place in a discussion of the land promises—especially in a discussion of the Pentateuch—I suppose one can understand this omission. The omission of Numbers, however, I found a little disappointing. After all, Numbers gets fledgling Israel from Sinai to the brink of the promised land. Moreover, ignoring Numbers means ignoring the journey motif so prominent in the Pentateuch. G. Wenham's body of work and D. Cole's relatively recent commentary demonstrate how prominent and central the journey motif is to the corpus, especially in Numbers. I think it would have been fascinating to see Martin incorporate these ideas and at least consider the implications—including eschatological ones—of thinking through the ideas of journey and land promises together. This expectation, of course, betrays my own biases and may not be fair. After all, the study is about land promises and not journey.

Furthermore, one immediately notices that *Bound for the Promised Land* skips the postexilic literature altogether, an omission that may be even more problematic than skipping Numbers. The postexilic prophets, for example (Haggai, Zechariah, Malachi, and possibly others), address the covenant people who have returned to the promised land yet face the reality of having no temple and then, subsequently, an inferior one. From this context comes important prophetic contributions about Israel's place among the nations. In Zechariah there is the issue of the heavenly realm drawing near to the earthly one as angelic messengers decorate the text regularly. I do think Martin does an excellent job in working through the "major prophets"—Isaiah, Jeremiah, and Ezekiel—but there is no getting around the fact that this selection means there is no consideration of postexilic contributions from the prophets.

Equally problematic is the omission of postexilic historical books. Is there no contribution to the thesis from Esther, which deals with the covenant community outside the promised land and without a temple for encountering the covenant God of their ancestors? Could there be a contribution to the thesis from Ezra and Nehemiah, which highlight an attempt to re-actualize the exodus event and return to former ways of encountering YHWH through temple, land, city, and practices? I would have liked to see Martin deal with these books' contributions to international and ethnic issues, especially in the sincere attempts but overall failures visible in Ezra and Nehemiah. I think these texts could have been useful in many threads of discussion, not least of all in developing the point that the Old Testament shows an inherent anticipation of future development and something new and greater in God's redemptive plan.

There are some noteworthy omissions of secondary literature as well. For instance, his discussion of the original kingdom present in the creation account (Gen 1–2) conveniently ignores the potential problem areas of chaos and evil foregrounded in classic works by such scholars as B. Anderson and J. Levenson. He also does not engage D. Block's work on the phenomenon of a deity-people-land relationship in the ANE. That is not to say that Martin places the Old Testament in a vacuum; but, there is a sense that *Bound for the Promised Land* does not take into account the larger ANE *milieu* to the extent that it should have, especially with the concepts of creation and land. I was most surprised that Martin does not engage R. Hays's *Echoes of Scripture in the Letters of Paul* (Yale University Press, 1989). Not only is this work one of the most important pieces of scholarship having to do with the use of the Old Testament in the New, but it also speaks directly to the issue of God's faithfulness to Israel in His redemptive plan as seen in the sum of the Pauline corpus.

Though there are some noticeable omissions, I still found *Bound for the Promised Land* highly informative and very well put together. Martin's hermeneutical treatment of texts is responsible and careful. His grasp of the relationship between the Old and New Testaments is exemplary. Martin most definitely demonstrates the developments of God's land promises both as a response to the loss of the kingdom in Gen 3 and as a concept growing in anticipation of something greater as it expands in the Old Testament Scriptures. In particular, his treatment of the eschatological developments of the land promises in the prophets is at the same time academically helpful and spiritually stirring. Overall, I would suggest that Martin's treatment of the Old Testament portions of his study is reverent, informed, exegetically sound, and well done.

Furthermore, although he omits *Echoes of Scripture*, Martin's New Testament portions display a robust engagement of works on the Old Testament in the New and a thorough familiarity with the hermeneutical issues revolving around this blossoming area of study. In good form, he fully clarifies his disagreements with other scholars and consistently provides an accurate representation of all views foregrounded for discussion. Surely not everyone will agree with all of Martin's conclusions about the New Testament portions of his study, but I doubt that he will receive any charges of misrepresentation. Furthermore, as an evangelical myself, I appreciate that the work is not bogged down with engagements of fringe and skeptical perspectives that give more credence to ideologies than the actual text. Martin's study is quintessentially a biblical one. It is, quite frankly, refreshing for this evangelical reader.

As I reflect on my own encounter with this new study, I heartily recommend this volume to serious students of Scripture who want to know their Bibles better. If there was no "whole-Bible biblical theology" on God's land promises prior to this book, then *Bound for the Promised Land* most certainly ensures that there is one now, and an important one at that. I am particularly impressed with its breadth of coverage and investigative depth in roughly 200 pages. As an instructor, I am already trying to find a way to work this volume into one of my courses, which may be the highest praise I can give a new study like this one. With this addition, the New Studies in Biblical Theology series by IVP continues to establish itself as one of the most important evangelical, academic series in the field. In a work of this scope, every scholar is going to find some omission(s); but, I am confident that there is plenty in this volume for anyone wanting to understand the organic relationship of the whole Bible better. Martin has provided a real treat for evangelicals. Enjoy it.

R. MICHAEL FOX
Ecclesia College

The Text of the Hebrew Bible: From the Rabbis to the Masoretes edited by Elvira Martín-Contreras and Lorena Miralles-Maciá. JAJS 13. Göttingen: Vandenhoeck & Ruprecht, 2014. 262 pp., €89.00, hardcover.

This is a solid collection of high-quality articles—written by a group of international experts—which serves both to clarify matters related to the Masora and to further research in the same field. The volume does not present a unified case; it rather offers various viewpoints which often complement each other but at times also convey contradictory opinions. An introductory chapter, written by the two editors of the volume, presents the state of research and highlights questions which are still waiting to be answered. One problem is the lack of adequate and shared terminology in the field of textual criticism; another one concerns the way in which rabbinic literature can or cannot be used to shed light upon the development of the Hebrew text. It is furthermore also clear that we know too little about the standardization and transmission of the biblical text prior to the Masoretes.

The rest of the volume falls in two parts. The first part contains six articles which explore the preservation and transmission of the Hebrew Bible. Emanuel Tov's article, aptly called "The Myth of the Stabilization of the Text of Hebrew Scripture," discusses the traditional scholarly claims in favour of a planned process toward the creation of a standard text. Rather, Tov argues, the fact that the MT ended up as the standard text is a matter of historical coincidence: the LXX had been turned into a Christian text, the Samaritan Pentateuch had become associated with the Samaritan community, and the Qumran scrolls were hidden and thus lost to the Jewish community.

John Van Seters explores the same issue but from a different perspective. He rejects the validity of a comparison between the preservation of the text of Homer and that of the Hebrew Bible. He also challenges Tov's aforementioned view. Rather, Van Seters claims, the development of the standard Hebrew text was governed by market forces: a text became canonical when it became well-known, and it was not always the best copies that were well-known. Instead, it could have been the cheapest ones that sold the best.

Arie van der Kooij continues on the same topic but focuses more on the people who copied the texts. Drawing from both the writings of Josephus and of the rabbis, van der Kooij argues that the priests in the temple were responsible not only for preserving the scrolls but also for their production.

Elvira Martín-Contreras summarizes the aims of her wider research project, namely to clarify and understand how the Hebrew text developed from the second temple period into what came to be known as the Masoretic text. Who were the *sopherim*, what did they do, and how were they connected to the Rabbis and to the Masoretes?

Günter Stemberger investigates the extent to which the rabbinic literature displays awareness of grammatical issues, such as matters related to grammatical gender and directive *he*, as well as how they relate to matters of varying orthography. He demonstrates that such awareness existed, yet it is rarely displayed. Furthermore, some of the relevant passages are probably later additions and thus cannot be taken as evidence.

Finally, the highly technical article by Julio Trebolle and Pablo Torijano explores the relationship between the textual variants of the LXX and how they agree or disagree with the variants of the MT in mediaeval manuscripts, with focus on the book of Kings. They conclude, among other things, that some of the variants in the Hebrew manuscripts may in fact be remnants of variants of the Hebrew *Vorlage* of the LXX.

The second part may be of less general interest as many of the six articles deal with complex technical matters and textual details. Nathan R. Jastram's short article is devoted to the so-called (now presumably lost) Severus Scroll, or rather to texts which testify to instances where this scroll displays variants from the MT. Jastram explores these recorded variants and how they compare with the ancient textual witnesses.

Alex Samely's substantial essay reflects on the nature of the information that the Masorah conveys and how it compares with the information transmitted by other types of Jewish literature from antiquity. In his article, Samely differentiates between meta-linguistic information, i.e., information which tells us about the linguistic constitution of a word (i.e., it contains so and so many letters), meta-textual information (concerned with the meaning of a word), and object-linguistic information (treating the word as an object and describing it as such). Samely concludes that the Hebrew Bible, the Mishnah, and texts know as rewritten Bible often convey information of the third kind, that the second kind is typical of the midrashic literature, and that the Masorah conveys nearly only information of the first kind.

Willem F. Smelik discusses the provenance of Targum Onqelos and Targum Jonathan: did they originate in the land of Israel or in Babylon? He highlights the often circular reasoning of taking the compilation of the Masorah as evidence of the location of the composition of the Targumim. Smelik examines the correlation between the *kethib* and *qere* in both eastern and western manuscripts of the MT with the reading of the Targumim, and concludes that this type of investigation is methodologically partly flawed and also fails to yield clear results.

Lea Himmelfarb's article shows a strong correlation between the Tiberian system of sentence division and accentuation and the earlier Babylonian systems. In 85 percent of the cases the later Tiberian system upholds the earliest Babylonian tradition of division and in 99 percent of the cases it upholds the later Babylonian tradition of division.

Yosef Ofer short study explores three enigmatic notes from the Babylonian Masorah relating to Gen 19:30, Exod 25:25, and Deut 4:31 and discusses and evaluates various ways of explaining them. In particular, he argues that the Babylonian Masorah employed not only biblical but also tannaitic Hebrew as the basis for its comments.

Finally, David Marcus argues for increased use of the Masorah in biblical research. Using the birth narrative of Samuel as a test case, he suggests three areas where the Masorah forms a useful supplementary tool for biblical interpretation: (1) to establish the parameters of a pericope, (2) to explore matters of intertextuality, and (3) to shed exegetical light upon a difficult passage.

In sum, this is a very fine and useful collection of articles for those scholars and lay-readers who are interested in the development of the biblical manuscript that we today consider to be authoritative.

LENA-SOFIA TIEMEYER
University of Aberdeen

Ruth by James McKeown. Two Horizons Bible Commentary. Grand Rapids, MI: Eerdmans, 2015. 162 pp., US $22.00, softcover.

James McKeown currently teaches Old Testament and Hebrew at Union Theological College, while also spending much of his time writing and teaching in church communities. He has previously published multiple articles concerning Old Testament studies as well as another commentary in the Two Horizons Series on Genesis. The Two Horizons Commentary series, of which his most recent commentary on Ruth is a part, is focused upon balancing close exegesis with the broader theological themes of a biblical book. McKeown's commentary on Ruth provides a much-needed perspective on the book, examining Ruth within its own context and within the context of the rest of the Old Testament canon.

The first half of McKeown's commentary is devoted to the expected exegesis and close reading of the book. McKeown begins by focusing on the importance of the book's language, drawing the everyday reader's attention to the fact that the book is full of coy wordplays and strategic repetitions in the Hebrew (p. 1). For this reason, McKeown provides the reader with the Hebrew script, a transliteration, and a translation of every word or phrase that he views as key to the book's meaning and literary play. This is one of the most helpful features of the commentary. It is a great boon to readers already familiar with Hebrew, and the transliteration provides a guide for those not familiar with the language. Rather than just providing Hebrew text throughout, discouraging lay readers, or only providing transliteration, frustrating scholarly readers, McKeown places the two side by side, allowing all parties to appreciate the slippery language that makes up Ruth. As for the rest of the introduction, McKeown provides short riffs on the standard questions of date, authorship, and genre (pp. 2–5) before going on to offer a brief synopsis of the narrative (pp. 5–11). He is quick to note the subtle ambiguity of the narrative, and in his own way he is ambiguous about answering some of the questions concerning date and genre. He points out that the setting of the book is in the period of the judges and often seems to read the book as history, even as he also concedes that the book's story/message would have fit better within the exilic/post-exilic time period (pp. 2–3). Again, noting that the genre seems to fit in with the historiographical narratives of Judges and Samuel, he also points to the book's strong connections with wisdom literature (p. 4). However, McKeown's ambiguity on these topics should not be seen as a downside; to the contrary, his recognition of the book's many tenuous ties and relationships is enlightening and sobering in the face of many who too often attempt to nail down every specific detail.

Throughout the commentary itself, McKeown again repeatedly highlights the ambiguous nature of the text and the way that it does not always allow us much insight into a character's motivations or the reasons for events (such as the death of Elimelech and his sons in Moab). Yet, despite his caution against other scholars reading too much into the texts, McKeown sometimes goes on to provide a possible explanation not supported by the text itself. For example, while discouraging scholars who postulate that Naomi implored Ruth and Orpah to return to Moab for her own sake rather than their sakes, McKeown claims that Naomi's urging was in fact entirely unselfish and motivated by her desire for the girl's best interests (p. 23). This is, of course, an entirely plausible reading of the story, but the ambiguity cuts both ways. The readings that he argues against on the basis of ambiguity are no more unstable than his own reading. Despite small moments like this, McKeown's exegesis is thorough, careful, and insightful throughout. When discussing the well-known declaration Ruth makes to Naomi when she is compelled by the older woman to return home, McKeown is careful to note that "this does not amount to a declaration of personal faith" (p. 26). Many commentators have argued that it certainly does or does not equal a confession of faith or a sign of proselyte conversion, but McKeown is willing to allow the subtlety of the text to stand as he plumbs the rich language of this declaration (pp. 25–30). Such careful and sharp exegesis pervades the commentary.

The second half of the commentary is devoted to the broader theological connections and implications within Ruth. In one section McKeown explores the book's relationship and shared theological themes with other books of the Old Testament (Genesis, Judges, Samuel, Job) as well as the theological implications of its characters and their actions within the narratives (pp. 71–110). Then, in a second section, McKeown probes the book's voice concerning more broad theological issues such as creation, providence, land, redemption, feminist questions, and missions. Both of these sections provide a breath of fresh air within studies of Ruth. Though many of these issues have been tackled by some scholars in individual articles, McKeown brings together questions of canonical context and theological themes in a brief and insightful format. His forays into these theological issues raised within and around the book of Ruth provide thoughtful answers and raise new and important questions, all while pointing the interested reader to more in-depth studies on each specific topic. This section alone would be worth purchasing, and yet its combination with the McKeown's detailed exegesis provided in the first half of the book causes the entire book to work together in an exciting way. The only downside to this broadly theological section is that McKeown often seems to be more specific (in order to answer some specific theological questions) in places where earlier he called for allowing the ambiguity of the text to reign. For example, in the second half of the book he seems to claim that Ruth's confession in 1:16–18 actually is a confession of proselyte conversion (p. 129). Or when discussing the issue of Ruth's disappearance from the end of the book, McKeown asserts, "From the standpoint of the book of Ruth the invisibility at the end of the book is compensated for by the title of the work, which does not allow us to forget that this is Ruth's story" (p. 101). Yet, I am not sure that a title assigned at a later time makes up for Ruth's invisibility in the face of patriarchal forces at the end of the narrative. Regardless, McKeown's specificity in these matters of ambiguity is understandable, as most theological questions require some semblance of concreteness; it is quite a challenge to maintain ambiguity while presenting theological clarity. These minor quibbles are brightly outshined by the book's brilliant combination of detailed exegesis alongside skilled theological exposition. Both the individual context of Ruth and the broader context of the Old Testament canon are brought to bear in a volume that is sure to be treasured by both scholars and lay readers alike.

RICHARD PURCELL
Emory University

Scribal Laws: Exegetical Variation in the Textual Transmission of Biblical Law in the Late Second Temple Period by David Andrew Teeter. FAT 92. Tübingen: Mohr Siebeck, 2014, xvi + 359 pp., US $110.00, hardcover.

Scribal Laws, by David Andrew Teeter, associate Professor at Harvard Divinity School, is a thorough revision and expansion of the author's 2008 Notre Dame dissertation, dedicated to his early teacher John H. Sailhamer. The central thesis of the book is that the variety of scribal phenomena (omissions, additions, updates, rearrangements, etc.) found in manuscripts of the legal portions of the Pentateuch "must be evaluated in the context of early Jewish scribal learning, exegesis, and thought. This scribal learning is characterized by conceptions of the text and language that differ significantly from the assumptions of modern philology and its procedures of discovering meaning, indicative of differences even in the fundamental structures of the knowledge and its cultivation" (pp. 198–99).

The book commences from two fundamental modern insights: 1) "that a variety of *exegetical* processes were operative in the scribal transmission of biblical texts" and 2) "that *legal* matters were among the foremost questions occupying exegetes at this time [i.e., the Second Temple Period]" (p. 1). Given that scribes altered or otherwise interacted with the texts they transmitted and that legal texts were of supreme interest to most ancient Jewish groups, Teeter seeks to discover the extent to which legal texts were intentionally changed and under what circumstances. The book's title is thus a double entendre as it explores "scribal laws" in the sense of regulations or rules governing scribal practice and also in the sense of legal material transmitted, composed, or influenced by scribes. The rest of chapter 1 explores the reality of textual plurality in the Second Temple period from the standpoint of the Dead Sea Scrolls and variants found in Greek manuscripts. Teeter situates the contemporary discussion of this data within the history of research, especially the early work of Abraham Geiger.

Chapter 2, "Exegetical Variation in the Text of Biblical Law," is an updated presentation of Teeter's doctoral thesis. The chapter is a long and highly detailed exploration, cataloguing, and analysis of most of the variants in the textual witnesses of the legal material of Exodus, Leviticus, Numbers, and Deuteronomy. The chapter is organized by size or length of a given expansion, divided into the following sections: Modern Expansions, Minor Expansions, Euphemism or "theological" Explication, Grammatical or Syntactical Resolution, Combined Expansion and Change, Change/Exchange, Word-Level (Lexical/Morphological), Letter-Level, Division (Phrase and Word), Combinations, and Exegetical Omission. The chapter includes several lengthy case studies including the issue of grazing/burning in Exod 22:4, seething a kid in its mother's milk in Exod 23:19, the famous relationship between the ritual and secular slaughtering regulations of Deut 12 and Lev 17, the so-called Samaritan ideological layer, and variants related to blood manipulation and the "base of the altar." The changes catalogued and discussed are contextualized vis-à-vis later rabbinic exegesis, early scribal practices in Egypt and Mesopotamia, and the insights of the nineteenth century *Wissenschaft des Judentums* movement (most notably Abraham Geiger). The chapter is lengthy, comprising nearly 40 percent of the whole book, and incredibly detailed.

Chapter 3, "The Textual Hermeneutics of Exegetical Variation in Biblical Law," is a relatively short, 25-page discussion focused on questions of the hermeneutics observable behind the textual variants. Central to Teeter's thesis is that understanding the Bible accurately (especially the legal material) requires that the modern reader forego common disciplinary assumptions (text-critical, philological, etc.) in favor of a more emic mindset—that of ancient Jewish readers and scribes. Teeter maintains that, following J. Koenig, ancient scribes worked by an analogical hermeneutic—nearly all of the data examined in chapter 2 can be explained in terms of scribes working from a verbal analogy, a graphic analogy, or a scriptural analogy. For example, Teeter cites the famous apparent contradiction of the Passover laws (pp. 195–96). Deuteronomy 16:7 requires that participants "boil" the lamb, while Exod 12:9 requires that participants eat the lamb "neither raw nor boiled in water, but roasted over fire." The larger analogy of Scripture—an early stage of canon-consciousness according to Teeter—can be seen to be at work in Second Temple sources that assume a corpus of scriptural works and their non-contradiction. Second Chronicles 35:13 describes Josiah's Passover as following *both* laws "they *boiled* the Passover lamp *in fire* according to the ordinance." The LXX of Deut 16:7 contains the addition of the verb from Exod 12, "you shall boil *and roast* and eat it," demonstrating similar scriptural consciousness, though providing a different exegetical solution to the commonly perceived problem. Teeter voices an opinion frequently stated by Eugene Ulrich: that at the very least we must recognize that the various conscious scribal changes would have been viewed or understood by the scribes and their community as legitimate handling of Scripture. Teeter points out that these changes, almost without fail, further the coherence and interconnectedness of Scripture. Thus, ironically to many moderns, the altering or changing of Scripture grows out of a dedication to its details and a pious notion of its ultimate harmony. Furthermore, the changes that occur are not no-holds-barred but rather dependent upon the contours or confines of the extant text. Scribal alteration was thus motivated by concern for the text and the many potential interpretations were limited by textual and social factors, the ultimate existence of textual pluriformity stems from "awareness of an interrelated, sacred scriptural whole" (p. 204).

Chapter 4, "Historical Assessment: The Nature and Background of Textual Variation in Scriptural Legal Texts," as the title declares, seeks to evaluate proposed explanations of textual variation. Returning to a question posed earlier in the study, whether legal ("halakhic") and non-legal ("aggadic") texts were handled differently, Teeter states that there is no evidence for special treatment of legal texts and that scribal changes are unrelated to genre. Instead, he claims that the two primary approaches found ("precise replication" and "expansionistic/facilitating") may have more to do with the type of manuscript in which the text is found, rather than geographical, social, or chronological factors.

Beginning with Gesenius in 1815, Teeter summarizes and evaluates the main proposals, assumptions, and explanations regarding the extant evidence of textual plurality. He discusses Gesenius, Frankel,

Kohn, Geiger, Kahle, Lieberman, Greenberg, Talmon, Kutscher, Cross, Tov, and Ulrich. Teeter concludes that evidence for early textual plurality and deliberate scribal intervention is now beyond doubt. Theories of vulgar texts, local texts, and the priority of the proto-MT as central or the provenance of "temple circles" all need to be abandoned or highly nuanced. Tov in particular receives some of the highest praise and the lengthiest critique, likely proportional to the sheer quantity and quality of his contributions to the subject. Following this survey of scholarship, Teeter points out the numerous problems in current definitions, labels, and categories (esp. vis-à-vis MT). His conclusions include the following observations: scribes were not a homogenous group; a "standard text" does prove "standardization" (i.e., purposeful directed movement towards uniformity); there is no proof of a "standard text" in the Second Temple period; "canonization" does not require textual stabilization or standardization; both "conservative and facilitating scribal models can be attributed to the influence of a scriptural collection . . . though neither is a necessary consequence thereof" (p. 254).

The final sections of chapter 4 address the issue of function for the "exact" and "facilitating" manuscripts. The Qumran evidence demonstrates that manuscripts of both types were coexistent, and other witnesses (SP, LXX, Chronicles, *Jubilees*, the *Temple Scroll*, 4QRP, etc.) show that these type of manuscripts were widespread. Past scholarship has almost unanimously presumed that manuscripts of the more expansive "facilitating" type were for popular use. Teeter argues persuasively to the contrary that the rewritten texts (e.g., *Jubilees*, *Temple Scroll*) clearly assume a learned audience who knows the details of the text. That these rewritten compositions as a rule utilize a more "facilitating" text as *Vorlage* is not because a "superior" text was not available, but, according to Teeter, because the choice of such a manuscript best served the interests of the authors. This (conscious) adoption of a "facilitating" *Vorlage*, says Teeter, is the only evidence for the function of the "facilitating" manuscripts, and it shows that they were taken seriously as authoritative scriptural manuscripts used by the learned for textually sophisticated readers. The question remains: how do the two scribal approaches ("exact" and "facilitating") relate? Did they serve the same functions in different contexts (e.g., local texts / vulgar texts) or did they serve different functions in the same context? The scholars surveyed in this chapter typically adopt the former option, and Teeter argues for the latter stating that manuscripts of both groups can be seen to have existed in the same time and location (Qumran) and thus a complementary function should be sought. Teeter finds an analogy for such a situation in the relationship of the MT to the Targumic tradition. Though the textual situation of the Second Temple period is not one of central authoritative text with secondary parallel versions, the Targumim (like the "facilitating" manuscripts) play more freely with the text and have in mind a scripturally knowledgeable readership (despite Rashi's and others opinions to the contrary). Fascinatingly, Teeter points out that the Targumim arise at essentially the very point in time where the widespread presence of "facilitating" manuscripts ceases, and in both cases "limited textual plurality . . . was not only tolerated, but actively embraced" (p. 267).

The brief conclusion reiterates that ancient assumptions about the text ("from inside") differ greatly from those of modern textual critics and philologists. Ancient scribes worked with "a supple notion of participation" informed by various types of analogy (verbal, graphic, scriptural, etc.). Understanding and explaining the reality of textual variation requires a step away from modern assumptions about what is "authentic," "preferable," or "secondary," and a step inside ancient scribal culture drawing on the full sweep of Biblical studies, Qumran studies, Jewish studies, and related fields—as the nineteenth century *Wissenschaft des Judentums* sought to do, seeing in the variants valuable evidence for earlier belief and practice (pp. 269–71).

I received a review copy of this book while teaching a graduate course on Pentateuchal Legal Codes as a Visiting Lecturer at the University of Wisconsin-Madison. As we translated most of the Covenant Code, Holiness Code, and Deuteronomic Code with special attention to textual and hermeneutical issues, the course provided an excellent setting for evaluating Teeter's catalogue and analysis in the second chapter. In hindsight, though Teeter makes "no claim to comprehensiveness" (p. 34 n. 1), his work is exemplary. For every detail or issue that I or my six doctoral students at UW explored, none were lacking in Teeter's analysis. Furthermore, Teeter's depth of engagement with modern scholarship, Second Temple sources, and rabbinic literature is stunning. The second chapter provides a (nearly?) exhaustive treatment of the textual variation within the legal material. This is clearly a book for specialists, but the value of the catalogue, the detailed treatments and analysis, and the extensive notes is immense and will not be overshadowed by any similar work in the near future.

The larger discussion of chapters 1, 3, and 4 show equal depth and care, situating the evidence of chapter 2 within the current scholarly discussion and the history of past research. Abraham Geiger is the recurring hero of the book from the introduction to its final conclusion, and it is primarily a return to his historical and cross-disciplinary approach that Teeter advocates throughout. Most central are the arguments for ancient analogical thinking about Scripture and for a complementary function of the "exact" and "facilitating" manuscripts.

While few of Teeter's claims are novel, he provides a thoroughly persuasive demonstration of the facts of ancient textual plurality, the unsoundness of attributing many LXX variants to the activity of the translator, and the need to understand ancient Jewish writings on their own terms.

JOHN F. QUANT
University of Northwestern–St. Paul

Textual Criticism of the Hebrew Bible, Qumran, Septuagint by Emanuel Tov. VTSup 167. Leiden: Brill, 2015, xxiv + 540 pp., US $218.00, hardcover.

This is the third volume of the collected works of Professor Emanuel Tov. Two earlier volumes of his collected studies were published in 1999 (Brill) and 2008 (Mohr Siebeck). This volume contains essays originally published between 2008 and 2014 (p. ix); the various chapters have all been reworked for the current volume, and in particular, bibliographies have been brought up to date, and cross references have been made to the other studies included in this collection.

The current volume reflects very well both the breadth and depth of Tov's work. The first, and largest, section is devoted to textual criticism of the Hebrew Bible; the second part is given to Qumran studies; and the final section focuses on the Septuagint. The three divisions of essays are not water-tight compartments isolated from one another. As is to be expected, there is a good amount of cross-fertilization between the three sections, but each section does reflect a major impetus and direction of Tov's work. The great variety of essays makes for a difficult review! But what will be attempted here is to review carefully the first article of section 1, and then more briefly review the most interesting essays of parts 2 and 3. It is hoped that this will encourage readers to consider carefully the rest of the volume as a way of gaining access to the contributions of Tov's wide-ranging scholarship.

The first section, devoted to textual criticism, is composed of 18 studies. The majority of them are presented in chronological order of appearance; two of the exceptions are review articles that are located at the end of the section. The first study, originally appearing in 2009, is titled "Reflections on the Many Forms of Hebrew Scripture in Light of the LXX and 4QReworked Pentateuch." This study is especially helpful in providing a window into Tov's current understanding of the history of the Old Testament text. Tov suggests that the most conspicuous feature of the MT may be its meticulous transmission over a period of 2000 years (p. 3). His discussion of the great similarity between texts dated near the turn of the era and the medieval manuscripts, including codex L and the Aleppo codex, is most helpful. He sees the preponderance of the MT as resulting from historical and sociological factors rather than the often hypothesized process of scribes standardizing the text through conscious activity (p. 5). When he speaks of the Samaritan Pentateuch, he describes it as being based on a text that was used previously in Judaism. Given the small number of pre-Samaritan texts that have been identified at Qumran, this may be an overstatement. At any rate, a fuller explanation would have been helpful. Toward the end of the initial section Tov speaks of the "acceptance [of the LXX] in Second Temple Judaism" (p. 7). I wonder if it might be better to speak of this as a partial acceptance in certain sectors or geographic areas where Jews found themselves residing.

The second section of the study is devoted to major content differences between the MT and the Hebrew parent text of the LXX. In this study Tov excludes books like Job whose major differences likely resulted from the activities of the translator(s) (p. 7). He likewise does not focus attention on LXX books like Jeremiah that reflect an edition preceding the MT. He discusses 3 Kingdoms (1 Kings), Esther, and Daniel, and he calls attention to the similarity in the character of these books to the "rewritten Bible compositions from Qumran" (p. 7). Differences between MT 1 Kings and LXX 3 Kingdoms include a greater emphasis on Solomon's wisdom, the addition of long theme summaries, dupli-cation of sections, and inclusion of an alternative version of Jereboam's reign alongside the original version (pp. 8–9). In regard to Esther, Tov prefers to speak of narrative expansions rather than the traditional "Additions A–F" (p. 9). In regard to Daniel, "the LXX changed, added, and omitted many details" (p. 10). The conclusion Tov draws from his study of these books is that they are similar to works found at Qumran such as 4QReworked Pentateuch (p. 13).

In the final section of this study Tov discusses issues of text and canon with regard to the three books examined in an earlier section alongside Qumran works such as 4QReworked Pentateuch. He distinguishes between an authoritative status within Judaism of the LXX versions of certain books, which he assumes as probable, and the question of whether the Hebrew and Aramaic originals of these books were also seen as authoritative within Judaism. In regard to the latter question, he sees it as "less certain" (p. 17). In the opinion of this reviewer, this final issue deserves much additional analysis to either support Tov's thesis or to reject it.

Part 2 consists of nine studies that focus on Qumran. They are presented in this volume in order of their previous publication. Two of the chapters merit special attention. In "The Sciences and the Analysis of the Ancient Scrolls: Possibilities and Impossibilities" Tov suggests that there are four areas where science can make a contribution. The date of the scrolls can be determined by measuring the age of the skin and the ink. Fragments from the same sheet may be identified through Carbon-14 analysis, DNA research, and the chemical composition of the skin. Previously unreadable letters may be recovered through new photographic techniques. And, finally, computer-assisted research may also help in discovering the relation between fragments (p. 268).

In "A Didactic and Gradual Approach towards the Biblical Dead Sea Scrolls" Tov discusses scrolls from sites other than Qumran, protomasoretic scrolls from Qumran, texts differing from the MT mainly in orthography and morphology, scrolls written in paleo-Hebrew script, pre-Samaritan scrolls and the SP, texts close to the Hebrew parent text to the LXX, and non-aligned texts. The chapter refers to 38 text samples, which can be found at http://www.sbl-site.org/assets/pdfs/pubs/DSS/Tov.pdf. There is much valuable material here, and its use along with the discussion in chapter 21 will yield much raw material that can be used so the reader may engage the world of the Qumran Biblical scrolls.

Part 3 contains six essays emphasizing the LXX, and all are presented in the order of their publication. Perhaps the most tantalizing of these works is titled "The Septuagint between Judaism and Christianity." In this chapter Tov speaks of the historical development of the LXX, especially how it was originally a Jewish endeavor but later was adopted by Christians. In a very intriguing analysis, Tov calls attention to the ways the LXX influenced the writing of the New Testament. He mentions the areas of language, terminology, theological foundations, and quotations (p. 455).

There is much to read and digest in this volume. It presents a fascinating assortment of the work of Emanuel Tov that was produced between 2008 and 2014. Readers will find much to ponder from the three major areas in which Tov has labored.

ELLIS R. BROTZMAN
Houghton, NY

Zechariah by Al Wolters. Historical Commentary on the Old Testament. Leuven: Peeters, 2014, li + 475 pp., US €74.00, softcover.

As necessary and useful as they are, biblical commentaries as a general rule make for very dull reading since their format is predictable and so much space is spent rehashing the views of previous scholarship that they quickly become repetitious; after consulting two or three commentaries on a given pericope they start to blur together. Wolters's contribution on Zechariah to the Historical Commentary on the Old Testament (HCOT) series is markedly different in this regard, for there is a freshness to its exposition which sets it apart and makes it a pleasure to read and consult.

As a commentary series, the HCOT does not seem strikingly novel in its approach, though it is written at a very high level of critical scholarship (the current volume boasts a 40-page bibliography on Zechariah, for example). Perhaps what will set the series apart for most readers of this journal is its distinctively European flavor, which is dominated by Dutch scholars and has very few American contributors. As a convenience, however, citations from non-English sources are given a translation as well. Theologically, the author identifies as an evangelical (pp. 2–3), and some of his perspectives in this volume will be more amenable to such a readership, particularly with regard to higher-critical issues. For instance, while he sees three major sections to the book (chs.1–6; 7–8; 9–14), he consciously departs from the common scholarly acceptance of its multiple authorship. While he does employ conventional terms such as "Second Zechariah" or "Deutero-Zechariah," he nevertheless accepts its overall unity (p. 22).

The author has had an eclectic professional background. His early career focused on the history of philosophy, beginning with a doctoral dissertation on Plotinus at the Free University of Amsterdam and then continuing at the Institute for Christian Studies in Toronto where he taught philosophy for a decade. His book *Creation Regained: Biblical Basics for a Reformational Worldview* (Eerdmans, 1985) is, just as the title indicates, focused on issues of Christian worldview in the Dutch Reformed philosophical tradition and has been a widely read text on the subject, appearing in a second edition in 2005 and being translated into several languages. Yet Wolters has also cultivated interests in Biblical Studies and later in his career went on to teach Bible and Greek at Redeemer University College in Ancaster, and he has extensive publications on topics relating to the NT, OT, and the Copper Scroll.

The author's diverse background is a strength, not a weakness, of the commentary, as it enriches his exposition at point after point. Wolters' chief interests lie in the areas of philology, history of interpret-tation, intertextuality, and Christian theological interpretation (p. 3), and these emphases are indeed borne out in the commentary. Some examples are mentioned herewith to give a taste of the work.

Wolters's attention to philology comes to fruition in oftentimes lengthy discussions of text-critical problems or lexical and grammatical issues. He views the MT with respect but does not view it as inviolate (pp. 9–10), and indeed, he is not averse to proposing fairly bold emendations at points. For example, in 8:11 he finds the text difficult and proposes a radically different reading of אַנְחִיל שְׁאֵרִית* (cf. v.12) in the place of the MT's אֲנִי לִשְׁאֵרִית (pp. 241–42). In this case the proposal is improbable, not only due to the lack of external support in Hebrew MSS or the versions but also because the syntagm is not problematic in the least, being well attested as an expression of possession. Similarly, his claims for enclitic *mem* in several instances (1:13; 5:6; 9:6; 11:7, 10; 14:5) will only be convincing to those who are inclined to accept it as a genuine phenomenon in Biblical Hebrew—a highly disputed topic—and in any event is certainly unnecessary for explaining the passages in question. On the other hand, at times his philological interest is particularly helpful. For example, along with others he correctly identifies an echo of Deut 28:1 in the conditional clause of 6:15b (cf. also Deut 11:13), but unlike many scholars he fully appreciates the syntactical implications of this, namely, that the introductory והיה is not to be understood as the apodosis (as it is translated, e.g., by the ESV) but rather as part of the protasis, as it is in its original context. He thus understands Zech 6:15b to be a case of aposiopesis or deliberately leaving a sentence unfinished (pp. 200–02). In many other instances that could be mentioned his attention to grammatical detail is similarly useful.

The example just mentioned also illustrates Wolters's emphasis on intertextuality. Although Zechariah's use of Scripture has been studied before in various works (e.g., Boda and Floyd, Wenzel, Stead), by its very nature it is an almost inexhaustible subject. Here too the commentary makes valuable contributions. For instance, when the prophet is directed to "take" (לקוח) some sort of offering from recently returned exiles in 6:9–15 in order to make a crown (or crowns) to serve "as a memorial" (לזכרון) in the temple, Wolters very plausibly suggests the influence of Exod 30:16 and Num 31:54, which also speak of the receiving of gold and silver for a memorial in the tent of meeting (pp. 183, 196).

The author's interest in the history of interpretation has already been evidenced with respect to Zechariah in previous articles and essays, such as an excellent survey on the צנתרות of 4:12 appearing in *Journal of Hebrew Scriptures*. In this commentary Christian interpretation from the patristic and Reformation eras, as well as Jewish interpretation from the rabbinic era to medieval scholars and contemporary Israeli exegetes, is judiciously brought to bear. In the course of his exposition of 2:10–17 [ET 6–13], for example, he surveys no less than 16 possible interprettations of the famous *crux* of 2:12 (pp. 80–82). This historical dimension does not prove a distraction but rather supports the exposition, particularly with a book such as Zechariah, which is filled with exegetical challenges.

The foregoing emphases culminate in Wolters's interest in Christian theological interpretation of Zechariah. For example, with regard to the mysterious figure of "the Branch" or, more accurately understood as a proper name, Ṣemaḥ (3:8; 6:12; cf. Arad 49:11), Wolters departs from many contemporary scholars who would identify him with Joshua the high priest and instead argues that he is a distinct future Messianic figure holding the offices of priest and king who is ultimately fulfilled in Jesus Christ (pp. 180–96). Thus he argues against the notion that Zechariah cultivates a diarchic system of leadership in postexilic Yehud shared between the priest and Davidic representative (in this he follows the work of Wolter Rose's *Zerubbabel and Zemah: Messianic Expectations in the Early Postexilic Period* [Sheffield Academic Press, 2000]). Yet his emphasis on theological interpretation is not uncritical, and he does not appeal to theological explanations as a way of dealing with difficult exegetical questions. For example, he departs from the views of Jerome, Luther, Calvin, and others in not identifying the angel of YHWH in 2:12 as being the second person of the Trinity (p. 84), even though it would simplify the exegesis to a certain extent.

All things considered, this is an outstanding commentary and a major contribution to Zecharian studies. One glaring weakness (presumably the fault of the series rather than the author) is the lack of indices (not even an index of Scripture references). This is to be corrected in future editions.

MAX ROGLAND
Erskine Theological Seminary

BOOK REVIEW INDEX

Celebrate Her for the Fruit of Her Hands: Studies in Honor of Carol L. Meyers edited by Susan Ackerman, Charles E. Carter, and Beth Alpert Nakhai (Reviewed by M. Sneed) 205

2 Samuel by Robert Barron (Reviewed by M. Y. Emerson) 208

For the Glory of God: Recovering a Biblical Theology of Worship by Daniel I. Block (Reviewed by J. M. Philpot) 209

The Artistic Dimension: Literary Explorations of the Hebrew Bible by Keith Bodner (Reviewed by D. J. Fuller) 214

Evil Within and Without: The Source of Sin and Its Nature as Portrayed in Second Temple Literature by Myryam T. Brand (Reviewed by L.-S. Tiemeyer) 216

Psalms in Their Context: An Interpretation of Psalms 107–118 by John C. Crutchfield (Reviewed by P. C. W. Ho) 219

YHWH is King: The Development of Divine Kingship in Ancient Israel by Shawn W. Flynn (Reviewed by D. S. Diffey) 221

Huldah: The Prophet who Wrote Hebrew Scripture by Preston Kavanagh (Reviewed by B. Stovell) 224

Ancient Israel's History. An Introduction to Issues and Sources edited by Bill T. Arnold and Richard S. Hess (Reviewed by K. van Bekkum) 228

Bound for the Promised Land: The Land Promise in God's Redemptive Plan by Oren R. Martin (Reviewed by R. M. Fox) 232

The Text of the Hebrew Bible: From the Rabbis to the Masoretes edited by Elvira Martín-Contreras and Lorena Miralles-Maciá (Reviewed by L.-S. Tiemeyer) 235

Ruth by James McKeown (Reviewed by R. Purcell) 238

*Scribal Laws: Exegetical Variation in the Textual Transmission
of Biblical Law in the Late Second Temple Period*
by David Andrew Teeter (Reviewed by J. F. Quant) 240

Textual Criticism of the Hebrew Bible, Qumran, Septuagint
by Emanuel Tov (Reviewed by E. R. Brotzman) 245

Zechariah by Al Wolters (Reviewed by M. Rogland) 248

www.ingramcontent.com/pod-product-compliance
Lightning Source LLC
Chambersburg PA
CBHW070925160426
43193CB00011B/1579